Euripides
Plays: One

Medea, The Phoenician Women, Bacchae

As Athens sank deeper into the twenty-seven-year war against Sparta she couldn't win, Euripides forced his fellow-countrymen to reconsider some of their most fundamental assumptions. In each of these three plays he portrayed individuals so incensed by injustice and grown so murderous in pursuit of redress that their actions can only destroy their families and spawn greater evil. *Medea*, *The Phoenician Women* and *Bacchae* are presented here in translations which are accurate and tested in production, with an introduction by Series Editor J. Michael Walton.

Euripides was born near Athens between 485 and 480 BC and grew up during the years of Athenian recovery after the Persian Wars. His first play was presented in 455 BC and he wrote some hundred altogether. Nineteen survive – a greater number than those of Aeschylus and Sophocles combined – including *Elektra*, *Hippolytos*, *Andromache*, *Ion*, *Alkestis*, and *The Women of Troy*. His later plays are marked by a sense of disillusion at the futility of human aspiration which amounts on occasion to a philosophy of absurdism. A year or two before his death he left Athens to live at the court of the King of Macedon, dying there in 406 BC.

EURIPIDES

Plays: One

Medea
translated by J. Michael Walton

The Phoenician Women
translated by David Thompson

Bacchae
translated by J. Michael Walton

introduced by J. Michael Walton

series editor: J. Michael Walton

METHUEN DRAMA

METHUEN DRAMA CLASSICAL GREEK DRAMATISTS

3 5 7 9 10 8 6 4

Methuen Drama
A & C Black Publishers Limited
36 Soho Square
London W1D 3QY

www.methuendrama.com

First published in Great Britain in 1988 by Methuen London Ltd
Reissued with a revised version of *Bacchae* 1998
This edition with a new translation of *Medea* published 2000

Medea translation copyright © J. Michael Walton 2000
The Phoenician Women translation copyright © David Thompson 1988
Bacchae translation copyright © J. Michael Walton 1988, 1998

This collection copyright © Methuen 1988, 1998, 2000
Introduction copyright © J. Michael Walton 1988, 1998, 2000

ISBN: 978 0 413 75280 2

Available in the USA from Bloomsbury Academic & Professional,
175 Fifth Avenue/3rd Floor, New York, NY 10010
www.bloomsburyacademicusa.com

A CIP catalogue record for this book
is available from the British Library

Typeset by Deltatype Ltd, Birkenhead, Wirral

CONTENTS

INTRODUCTION

There are two reasons for studying the history of the theatre. One is historical, the other theatrical. The plays of any period and the theatre for which they were written offer a special insight into the nature of a civilisation, its ideas and its preoccupations. Were it not so, drama could make no claim to being an independent discipline deserving study at the highest level. An individual play is something in addition. Once it was a performance piece. If it cannot talk to new generations of audience, it may as well stay on the shelf; no dishonourable place perhaps, but, for a play, the equivalent of being put out to grass in decent but ineffective retirement.

Greek tragedy spent the best part of two thousand years confined to the ivory tower with only the most sporadic of forays into the marketplace. The last hundred years have seen these forays become regular, though hardly routine; but seldom has the state of the theatre, nor the state of the world, seemed more opportune for a reappraisal of the theatre of the Greeks. And of all Greek plays, none seem so modern as those of Euripides.

The Athenian theatre derived its form and its impetus from the special circumstances under which it operated. The plays are powerful pieces. They can speak for themselves. But an informed account of the background to their first performance must throw light on the dramatic method and iron out some of those factors which for so long made Greek tragedy appear inaccessible to the ordinary playgoer. This is especially true of Euripides, much of whose work served as a challenge to what the audiences of his own time had come to expect.

In the spring of 431 BC Euripides' *Medea* was produced at the Great Dionysia in Athens. As was customary, each of three tragedians presented four plays in competition. None of the other eleven plays has survived, but the record shows that the group which included *Medea* was placed last. More than twenty years later – the date of *The Phoenician Women* is uncertain, though 409 BC seems likely – Euripides was more successful, coming second with the set from which his 'Theban' play has survived. The *Bacchae* was almost certainly produced in Athens in 405 BC. *Iphigenia at Aulis*, from the same group, is also extant and this time Euripides was successful in winning first prize. This can hardly be regarded as a consolation for previous disappointment, as he had already been dead for a year. The posthumous *Bacchae* was not the playwright's only victory in the dramatic competitions. He had four 'firsts' to his name while alive, but four seems niggardly in a working life of fifty years.

Only two months after *Medea* in 431 BC, Attica was invaded by Archidamus, King of Sparta, and the Peloponnesian War between Athens and Sparta began in earnest. It was to last intermittently for twenty-seven years and end with total defeat for the Athenians the year after the *Bacchae*. These two plays serve as a frame for a war which demolished Athens' empire and almost her civilisation. *The Phoenician Women* was in the thick of it, between a civil war in Athens itself and Euripides' departure into self-imposed exile in Macedon, where he spent his last years at the court of King Archelaus.

So varied are the plays that have come down to us that generalisations about Greek tragedy or comedy are almost always misleading. What does seem unarguable is that the function of the playwright in society was accepted by the Athenians as a didactic one and that, if Euripides was unable regularly to commend himself to the festival juries, it was largely because his message was too disturbing for these war-torn years. Times of hostilities are in most civilisations the least productive of periods for serious drama. Despite this, and despite reservations at the time about Euripides' work, in Athens of the fifth century BC war seems to have served as a positive stimulus.

The work of four major Athenian playwrights survives, discounting the meagre helping of Menander's new comedy written a century after the death of Euripides. Aeschylus died in 456 BC, having lived and worked through the defeat of the Persians at the battles of Marathon and Salamis and the sometimes painful birth of the new democracy. Seven of his plays survive, the same number as of Sophocles, born thirty years after Aeschylus, who grew up to defeat him in competition and outlive even Euripides. Nineteen plays are attached to Euripides' name. One is a problematic attribution; another not a tragedy, but a satyr play performed as a comic afterpiece to three tragedies. The surviving tragedies of this 'unpopular' playwright still outnumber those of Aeschylus and Sophocles combined. Aristophanes, the supreme comic writer of the fifth century, whose 'old comedies' represent a genre in their own right, was barely fourteen when the Peloponnesian War began, and all but two of his surviving eleven comedies were played before the defeat by Sparta.

The curious conclusion from all this data is that of the forty-four plays which comprise the corpus of classical drama, the seven of Aeschylus date from the early part of the fifth century BC. Of the remaining thirty-seven, more than thirty have the Peloponnesian War as a backdrop. In few of these is war seen as anything but hateful. In tragedies such as the *Hecuba* or *The Women of Troy* of Euripides, the degrading effects on victor and vanquished alike could only have been seen as a comment on the behaviour of the Athenians, no less than the Spartans, during the current hostilities. Sophocles is less outspoken, but Aristophanes weighs in with absurdist visions of the God of War pounding the Greek states in his mortar in *Peace* and of bellicose Athenian and Spartan males reduced through sexual deprivation to rampant pacifism in *Lysistrata*. Through year after year of campaigns and battles, major writers risked accusations of defeatism, treachery even, by persisting in questioning the conduct of a war which every year Athens looked less likely to win.

But if the war could never be eliminated from the sensibilities of his audience, or the audience of any other playwright of the time, Euripides pointed to other truths about the human condition which were so unpalatable that it was not until after his death that audiences were prepared to stomach them. Not all his plays are about war widows and the pointless waste of young life decked out as martyrdom. He wrote of the power of the passions, the arbitrariness of fate and the ambiguity of motive. So did Aeschylus and Sophocles, but Euripides did more. He debunked reputations, mortal and divine. He pinpointed hypocrisy and exposed its disguises. Medea murders her children, but she is driven to the act by male callousness. The combined efforts of the entire family of Oedipus cannot prevent his two sons killing one another and dragging the whole world into their mutual loathing. Pentheus is dismembered by his mother, both of them victims of a life force they have tried to deny. Passion is irresistible. The internal war for Euripides was as mad and destructive as the external.

All the Greek tragedians are absorbed by strength and weakness. Euripides matches the others in this, but in this world strength and weakness are deceptive, human characters more circular than polarised. His weapon is surprise. Nothing appears to him to be more fun than leading an audience down the path of his moral garden and then up-ending them on to the compost heap. Heroines prove tartars, sinners find a bit of halo to polish. His paradoxes can be as bizarre as those of Aristophanes, as thought-provoking as those of Brecht.

The greatest paradox of all is that Euripides should have been creating his subtle dishes from a recipe whose ingredients at first sight appear so unpromising. The physical conditions that dictated the nature of the Greek theatre seem appropriate to the powerful theatrical stroke and the unequivocal statement, but hardly to the nuances of sub-text. Perhaps this was another reason for the shock with which audiences reacted. But one thing is sure, Euripides knew precisely what he was doing, and dramatic effects, including those identified by critics centuries later, can with some confidence be ascribed to the playwright's design. This is not to suggest that he could or would have subscribed to all the theories propounded about his plays, still less claimed paternity to the wilder aberrations perpetrated by some modern directors. It does mean that he created drama which was ahead of its own time and better suited than that of his contemporaries to the twentieth-century mind.

The physical conditions that obtained in the Athenian theatre in the fifth century BC are open to dispute. This is both a blessing and a curse; a blessing because it continually licenses scholars to speculate and practitioners to create; a curse because the temptation for both to disregard the perspective of the other has resulted in the relegation of the classical repertoire to the lower divisions, with only the occasional cup-run to stimulate season-ticket holders. If such a sporting metaphor appears strained, let it be defended by reference to the sense of occasion which overlaid the whole process of play production in classical Athens, with the same civic significance given to dramatic as to other festivals, including the athletic.

It is customary, and right, to draw special attention to the religious nature of Greek festival. The occasions devoted primarily to dramatic performance took place during the winter or early spring: the Lesser or Rural Dionysia in a variety of locations during December; the Lenaia, at which comedy was featured, in January; and the Great or City Dionysia in March or the beginning of April. This latter was the festival for which the plays of Aeschylus, Sophocles and Euripides were written, as well as some of the plays of Aristophanes. The Great Dionysia included processions and proclamations, sacrifices and ceremonies as well as the three sets of tragic plays and four or five old comedies, all in the space of at most six days. The god Dionysos presided, his statue escorted into the theatre as part of the opening ceremony and taken back to its shrine on the road to Eleutherai at the conclusion. Dionysos was always God of the Theatre from the first introduction of dramatic performance into the festival of the Great Dionysia, generally accepted as about 534–530 BC. By this time the festival, inaugurated by Peisistratos some twenty-five years earlier, was well established, though the Dionysiac religion had not made an appearance in mainland Greece until fairly late, later certainly than the twelve Olympians who form the Greek pantheon and periodically interfere with the mortal world in *The Iliad* and *The Odyssey*. Passages of these two epics of Homer were recited at the Great Dionysia both before and after the introduction of dramatic production.

Dating for any events in the pre-classical period is at best hazy, but the war against Troy provided a convenient hitching-post for myth. Most of the heroes could relate at least their genealogies to the ten-year siege by the Greeks seeking the return of Helen and the ten-year period after Troy's sack which it took Odysseus to reach his home in Ithaca. Historically this razing of Troy is believed to have occurred about 1200 BC. As Homer was probably not creating or compiling his poems until four hundred years later, and it was another three hundred years before anyone began to think of writing history, what is remarkable is not so much the contradictions as the fact that there should have been any kind of coherence at all.

The Greek tragedies did for the most part relate to a world that really had existed, though some of the more grotesque figures seem the progeny of nightmare rather than folk memory. The *Bacchae* probably does record the arrival in Northern Greece of an eastern deity whose properties were disruptive and hence opposed, but who eventually caused the destruction of the young King. Pentheus is the grandson of Kadmos, founder of Thebes. This is the same Kadmos whose great-great-grandson, by a more durable if hardly better-starred line, is Oedipus. Heracles, the best known of all Greek heroes, had a connection with Thebes through a marriage to Megara, daughter of Creon, the uncle/brother-in-law of Oedipus. Heracles provides a link, if peripherally, to both the Trojan War and the expedition of the Argonauts which resulted in Jason bringing Medea to Corinth. To compound confusion, it is Creon's daughter for whom Jason jilts Medea, but, as King of Corinth, he is a different Creon from the Creon who becomes King of Thebes. The Greek stage world does consist of a seeming pool of wandering characters – Theseus is another – who happen in from time to time, rather as though they were Pirandellian creations waiting for a cue to enter the play, any play.

When they lived and what they really were is not in itself discernible or important. What *is* important is that the world of myth was a confused and swirling one, not dissimilar to that of King Arthur, or even the Lear and Macbeth of the English and Scottish Dark Ages. As Shakespeare latched on to the names and gave them dramatic substance for the audience of Jacobean England, so Euripides enjoyed the freedom of ready-made figures, whose given qualities consisted less of fixed characteristics than of specific deeds. It was the circumstances surrounding them which were his raw material. Gods as well as humans were liable to find their motives questioned. Dionysos himself was not exempt at his own festival in his own theatre, and in front of his own statue.

Every aspect of the Greek dramatic festivals seems geared to creating an occasion when religious observance became fully integrated with civic ritual. The theatrical power generated fuelled both the individual and the corporate need. The ability of playwright and performer to rouse emotion was the means by which the audience assessed a play, but the occasion made the theatre doubly dangerous. On the one hand, the temper of the times was on display. On the other, the theatre was a place which seethed with new ideas. When characters were forced to face realities, so were the audience. If a general warning against excess was the message reduced to its simplest, it was a moral banged home with startling frankness.

Whether the ultimate aim was to exercise or exorcise the emotions so roused was all one to Plato, who would have none of it in the ideal state he proposed in his *Republic*. Plato shared with the Pentheus of the *Bacchae* an instinctive appreciation of the power of Dionysos. To puritans, both then and since, the theatre represents a threat. Its instinct is for the subversive. The more sensitive the times, the more alarming the frankness of a Euripides must seem.

An Athenian audience was large. The auditorium of the theatre for which Euripides wrote, as renovated by Pericles, must have held at least seventeen thousand. Today the amphitheatre at Verona might offer an audience a comparable experience, but even that resembles more the Greek theatre of the fourth century, when individual performance overshone content. Comparisons with modern pop concerts or football matches are actually misleading, and the evangelist meeting, where emotion smothers reason, offers no proper parallel to the promotion of rational argument through highly charged example, which is the mark of the Athenian drama. Only in the East might it be possible to find a tradition in which the world of the spirit still relates art to life, extolling the community it informs.

This is not to suggest that a modern audience has been disinherited from the Greek canon, only that there are pitfalls. Reconstruction of the original conditions of performance could never be more than an academic exercise with the single purpose of providing an insight into how and why playmakers of a past period made plays as they did. It may answer questions relating to stages and scenery, to costume and convention, to buildings and bank balances, actors and audiences. Some of these conditions may even be artificially recreated. Others cannot, notably the audience, whose expectations contribute enough to a performance to render the period replica vapid. No, the whole exercise revolves around the search that a modern director must undertake for equivalents which are properly rooted in the original material. If no precise analogue might seem to exist for a masked actor intoning strict verse to a musical accompaniment before a dancing Chorus and an audience of seventeen thousand ancient Athenians, then let the director look to essences and recall that the finest theatrical minds of the last hundred years have all seen the theatre as a synthesis of other art forms, overlaid with something that is unique to the theatre. Whether they did so consciously or not, Craig, Reinhardt, Meyerhold, Brecht, Artaud and Brook have all returned to the theatrical priorities of Aeschylus, Sophocles and Euripides.

All this is for the directors of these plays, and for the readers too, who should not be allowed to assume, because words are what have survived, that Euripides' art is a wholly literary one. The nature of the occasion was clearly one factor affecting the plays' form. Another was the physical aspect of the theatre and the way in which it related to a series of performance conventions. It was out of these conventions, which at first sight might appear to be at odds with his material, that Euripides was able to fashion his distinctive dramatic style. The earliest form of tragedy featured a chorus and a single actor. Whether this actor had ever been one of the chorus is less clear, but the choral element – that is, dance and song – remained central to the whole performance throughout the classical period. Aristotle, in the *Poetics*, confirms an impression which the plays point to: that Aeschylus introduced a second actor, Sophocles a third. The chorus numbered twelve or fifteen for tragedy, twenty-four for comedy. These norms did not restrict the number of characters to two or three, of course, and a secondary chorus was used on occasions, as well as a large number of supernumeraries. But there was no regular fourth 'actor' and the Euripides plays which survive can comfortably be performed by a company of three speaking actors. It is possible that the received manuscripts include emendations geared to suit the touring system of the fourth and third centuries BC. Sorting out exactly what may or may not be original Euripides has been a critical exercise for centuries, but, as in the long run it boils down to scholarly preference, we would be advised to accept the authenticity of what we have, unless it simply fails to make sense. In addition to the three actors, *Medea* has parts for two children, who appear with their mother and later call for help off-stage. *The Phoenician Women* has a cast of eleven, apart from the Chorus, which is a lot to divide amongst three performers, but can be done. The *Bacchae* is straightforward enough, as long as one can accept the actor who plays Pentheus later returning as his own mother Agauë, brandishing her son's head (or mask) on her Bacchic wand.

The question *why* the Greek playwrights should have restricted themselves to a limited number of actors is a different matter and has received a variety of answers. The more compelling relate to money. By Euripides' time, actors, though not chorus, were professionals and were allotted by the state to each playwright whose submission of plays had been accepted for festival production. Other expenses, with the exception of the theatre fabric managed on a commercial basis by the *architekton*, were the responsibility of an individual citizen, who had little choice about subsidising the state in this or some similar enterprise. This *choregos* equipped a production to certain standards. Paying for one or more extra actors, as seems to have been essential for some of the comedies at least, may well have been beyond the pocket or inclination of some sponsors, especially as they had to costume the entire production and pay a choreographer, perhaps also a director.

The Greek actor was not, as is now generally agreed, the grotesque figure of Hellenistic or Roman times. Those infamous 'high boots', so beloved of the compilers of potted histories of the theatre, are not of the fifth century BC at all, and every visual representation of the tragic mask from contemporary vase-painting suggests realism rather than exaggeration. The *cothurnus* was worn by the tragic actor, but it was a soft knee-length boot with no platform sole. By the time of Euripides, costume seems to have possessed some formal elements, depending on character, but was based on everyday dress of the time – the *chiton* or tunic which was pinned at the shoulder and a *peplos* or cloak where appropriate. Rank or profession could be signified by specialist costume, by colour or by what was carried. Many characters could be identified simply by appearance. Armour, a traveller's hat, winged sandals, a suppliant's offerings, lionskin and club, trident, thyrsos, mourning robes, old men's staffs – all conveyed meaning. Euripides was reputed to have first moved in the direction of realism with his portrayal of the beggar-king Telephos as more beggar than king, but the principal weapon of the actor puts this realism into perspective. That weapon was the mask and, however 'real' the mask, masked acting is not realistic.

The mask could vary in colour and in aspect – darker for a man, lighter for a woman. There were specialist masks for some of the grosser characters, or, for example, for the blinded Oedipus. In comedy there were portrait masks, but, natural or monstrous, the wearing of masks dictates a way of acting with which few modern performers are familiar or comfortable. Masked acting is a precise and definite means of translating speech into physical expression. The language of gesture, *cheironomia*, was the true language of the Greek theatre, serving to point and promote both speech and song. The extent to which the chorus danced mimetically can never be known, but the range of emotions they were called upon to portray and the scope of the actions they describe cannot but read to the theatre practitioner as choreographic instruction. Attempts have been made, if sporadically, to recreate this choreography from metrical pattern. The shared rhythm of certain lyric passages suggests that the principal actors too could at times be classified as much dancers as actors. With accompanying music from double pipe, possibly lute and percussion, all but lost, the total nature of Greek performance must remain conjectural. What the mask demands of the actor can be pinned down, if only because of the universality to be found among those theatre traditions, mainly oriental, in which the mask is still the centre of the performance. The voice was clearly important to the Greek actor – Sophocles reputedly gave up performing because his was too weak for a massive open-air theatre – and audiences were used to listening closely to argument in the Athenian Assembly. But to ignore the physical dimension of Greek performance is to defy the tradition from which acting sprang.

When it comes to the shape of the theatre and the settings used to identify location the waters are again murky. The Periclean theatre in Athens, that is the Theatre of Dionysos as it was modified in the second half of the fifth century BC, possessed a scenic background, or *skene*, which was wooden. This much is known with some certainty. A hundred years later it was replaced by the first stone facade. A wooden *skene* could imply no more than the most meagre of backings for the actor, with a place to enter from and exit to that did not involve the long walk right out of the theatre which the chorus had to use. The precinct offered an arena of three separate but interconnected spaces: the *skene* with an acting area in front; the *orchestra*, or dancing-place; and the *theatron*, for spectators, with seats following two-thirds of the perimeter line of the orchestra. For the most part the three groups – actors, audience, chorus – kept to their own place, with the actors playing in a shallow plane before the *skene*. The chorus did sometimes encroach onto this area and the actors clearly made the odd inroad into the *orchestra*, while all performers could use the *parodoi* between *theatron* and *skene* for entrance and exit.

Most Greek plays are set in front of a house or a palace, as are *Medea*, *The Phoenician Women* and *Bacchae*. Others are not, a few requiring a change of location from scene to scene in the same play. Wooden stages unfortunately disappear without trace, and though vase paintings can again be helpful in sorting out theatrical conditions, those which may be inspired by dramatic scenes were never intended as 'production photographs'. The outstanding question is whether any additional stage-settings were employed. 'Actual locale and any variation from the stock exterior can be assumed from the spoken word,' runs one argument. 'On the contrary,' runs another, 'Sophocles is credited

by Aristotle with inventing *skenographia*, and that can only mean
"scene-painting".' Certainly there is solid evidence for the use by
Euripides' time of the *ekkuklema*, a wheeled platform for the
display of tableaux, and the *mechane*, or stage-crane, for the
revelation of gods. These pieces of machinery did not add to a
realistic effect – they would hardly have done that – but did
extend the range of spatial and visual possibilities. The strongest
advocate of the 'empty space' cannot deny that the Greek theatre
was not simply a place of the imagination. The argument for
individual design features – a raised stage, porch units, painted
panels and properties at the very least – is hard to resist, but can
never be taken as proved. It is perhaps not unfair to add that the
greater the devotion of the critic to language and the spoken
word, the less he or she seems to see a need for staging devices.

The strange and intriguing aspect of any such disputes is that
the bare bones of Athenian stage practice are sufficiently clearly
defined for solution to specific staging issues to prove largely
irrelevant in identifying how Euripides manipulated audience
expectation. The Greek theatre was at all times an artistic
conglomerate rooted in artifice. Like other art forms it was built
up in layers. These layers involved ways of seeing. They involved
levels of understanding. This was a theatre of example and
parable. Touching reality only at a tangent, it was at its most
powerful and poignant when creating its own world from which
the audience could draw their own conclusions. Tragedy may not
have been invented by Aeschylus, but for us today he defined it,
examining the plight of a Prometheus or an Orestes in grand,
passionate terms. Sophocles brought man to the centre, man at
the level of hero, however flawed: Ajax or Oedipus. Euripides
received the myths from the past and his theatre from Aeschylus
and Sophocles. What he could not do was reconcile the old
stories with the human condition as he saw it. So with the
framework of a heroic theatre, he took his heroic characters and
made them behave like people. Sometimes they seem sadistic,
sometimes comic, often truly pathetic. The audience were
confronted with the theatre they knew – acting-areas, masks,
chorus, everything they understood the theatre to be. The
characters still spoke in verse, but what they talked about were no

longer abstract ideas or the conflict of ideals. They sounded real, and that made people uncomfortable. Now in the twentieth century they still sound real and they still have something to say to us.

All they need is a means, but that ought not to prove a problem in a contemporary theatre, more aware than at any time in its history of the full range of modes of expression. The danger of promoting the form at the expense of the content is, of course, a real one, and for this reason, if for no other, Euripides deserves to be read in versions as close as possible to the received manuscripts. If some references seem at this range to be elusive or simply quaint, then that is to be expected, and any director is at liberty to adapt to suit the audience. What should and can shine through is the kind of blazing honesty about human beings and the world they live in that makes a nonsense of the 'barrier' of two and a half thousand years. The Athenians knew they needed their theatre. We should be in no doubt that our theatre needs Euripides.

Medea

> What gift of the gods could be finer for man
> Than to raise up his hand o'er the head of his foe,
> Triumphant?   *Bacchae* (*ll.* 878–880)

So sing the Chorus of Asian Bacchants relishing the prospect of Pentheus' humiliation and death for opposing the god Dionysos. A modern audience, holding, however notionally, to Christian ideals of charity and compassion, may wince when confronted by such a single-minded impulse to revenge. An Athenian one would have seen nothing wrong in retaliating for injury sustained, though the ensuing complications are at the heart of almost all tragic situations. Euripides was not the first of the Greek tragedians to use this apparent contradiction to force an audience to take stock of its moral stance and perhaps to adjust it, but with him it becomes almost an end in itself. By a curious reversal, the initial conflict in *Medea* is one where sympathy for the wronged heroine is greater today than it would have been in fifth-century BC Athens, where Euripides was regarded, if Aristophanes is anything to go by, as something of a misogynist. Euripides, so modern in his sympathies, had to ensure that even an audience of Greeks would have been hard put to it to approve of this Jason.

In the first of his confrontations with the wife he is in the process of ditching in order to marry the King of Corinth's daughter, Jason coldly and rationally sums up the relationship with Medea as he sees it. In the first place Medea was quite unable to prevent herself helping Jason because of her love for him. He graciously allowed her to accompany him back from the wastes of Colchis to civilisation, where her gifts are more widely appreciated. His new marriage will be to the advantage of his and Medea's children, offering them security. Medea is wrong to get upset because of the interruption of their relationship. But, there, that's women.

The indignation that such sentiments naturally arouse today might suggest that *Medea* is an easy play. It is certainly a popular one, with more new productions in recent years, in a variety of production styles, than any other Greek tragedy or comedy, not to mention adaptations from Anouilh to Dario Fo. The original, though, does present some problems which will not simply evaporate by treating the play as a propagandist tract.

The opening is straightforward. The first character to appear is the Nurse, who reminds the audience of the circumstances which led to Jason and Medea arriving in Corinth. Jason has now betrayed Medea and she has reacted against him with a passion as powerful as that she formerly demonstrated in his interest. The Nurse is clear that Jason is in the wrong. She feels sympathy for Medea, though the power of her mistress's temper appals her.

The Tutor joins her, accompanied by the two children of Medea and Jason. Nurse and Tutor wag their heads at men's selfishness, as Medea is heard lamenting off-stage. The Chorus arrive, again sympathetic, again uncomfortable at Medea's extravagant reaction. By the time Medea does enter, her weeping has been replaced by an intensity that is far more chilling. It takes Creon, among the play's characters, to show any real awareness of Medea's true strength, and in the face of it he succumbs to her plea for time.

When Creon leaves the scene, the Chorus almost unwittingly

find themselves accomplices in a course of action which is to lead to four murders, the last two infanticides of desperate savagery. This is not Medea's initial plan. Her first reaction is to kill Jason and his new wife, and she draws the Chorus in 'in celebration of women', as fellow victims of men. They identify their allegiance even before Jason has put in an appearance. When he does arrive, every word he says reinforces the dislike that an audience must feel for him. By the time he offers Medea letters of introduction to some of his friends, Euripides has almost made him a figure of fun, in the grisly black kind of way that will eventually see Pentheus as the butt of Dionysos in the *Bacchae*. How can anyone be so blind as Jason, an audience might muse, at least half aware of how many of their acquaintances can be just as obtuse, if in less extreme circumstances? And, as when Pentheus berates Dionysos in the *Bacchae*, anticipation of the victim's revenge adds relish.

At this point the Chorus sing a surprisingly bland ode about the difficulties of falling in love and the misery of being a refugee. It is, though, more than an interlude to pass the time. There is a turning point here for the Chorus, still not aware (though the audience are beginning to realise) precisely where their natural sympathies are leading them.

The next scene tightens the knot. Out of the blue, Aegeus arrives from a visit to the oracle of Apollo. This sudden intervention from someone who can provide Medea with a bolt-hole has met with critical scorn over the years. Certainly there is no preparation for Aegeus' arrival and it is all too patently a matter of convenience for Medea and plot. But there is point to the scene which a whole view of the play brings out. Medea offers to help Aegeus over his childlessness in exchange for protection. Cautiously he agrees, on condition that she can make her own way to Athens.

Only when the play has run its course does it become apparent that this scene is more than a device for tying up ends. Aegeus' behaviour to Medea is on a par with that of everyone else; main characters, Chorus and probably audience. He is quite happy to appear to wave a liberal flag as long as it involves him in doing as little positive as possible, and if there is something in it for him.

Aegeus, King of Athens as the audience are reminded, is a model of feckless diplomacy, our contemporary diplomacy no less than Athenian.

At the end of the play Medea appears to have extracted herself from her immediate situation by acquiring divine protection. She mentions in passing that she intends to settle in Athens, but by this time witch has become both seer and demi-goddess and is more than capable of looking after herself. The episode with Aegeus may seem isolated to someone attempting to apply to *Medea* the structure of a well-made play. Greek tragedy is seldom 'well-made'. Euripides is not alone among the Greeks in directing attention towards an issue from a series of perspectives. His *The Phoenician Women* offers a parallel, but others can be found in Aeschylus' *Prometheus* or Sophocles' *Oedipus at Colonus*. In each, the playwright builds a picture, the complete impression of which is of greater importance than an integrated plot. Because Euripides deals in reversals and recognitions in a manner that even Aristotle, no admirer of the *Medea*, would have acknowledged, detractors have been tempted to treat him as a simple story-teller, who worked himself into corners and who then extricated himself by damaging the story he was telling. Such a verdict is facile.

The practitioner, working on the production of a Euripides play, discovers soon enough that the purpose is not to manufacture a Chekhovian world in which any character is as interesting as any other. Myth dictated the outlines of the plot. What was fresh in Euripides was a determination to promote understanding. This is why his central figures can speak and react with real emotions, allowing the audience to be led gradually to see what motivates actions beyond their immediate comprehension. Medea murders her own children. How do you account for such an action? Euripides makes it possible not so much by enlisting sympathy for her crime as by forcing the audience to contemplate the circumstances in which it came to pass. Aegeus is as much a part of the 'civilised' world as is Jason, or indeed the Chorus, and his scene fits another piece in the jigsaw.

Only after he has departed does Medea reveal to the Chorus that her plan includes the murder of the two boys. Revenge against Jason, which was initially aimed at causing pain to him, and his new wife, has veered off in another direction. It is a jolt for the audience who have so far been able to treat Medea with undiluted sympathy. 'Very well,' says the playwright, 'put your money where your mouth is and see if you are still so sure of your moral superiority.' The Chorus are caught in the same dilemma. So far they have gone along with Medea's plans. Now they are victims of the trap which catches most Greek choruses, though not often with such drastic consequences. They cannot get away until the play is over. No longer can they sit on the fence and sympathise with some hysterical threat. Either they inform on Medea, or they become accessories before the fact. In the hands of Euripides a convention becomes a moral pivot. Nor do they have long to think about it. After a brief ode in which they beg Medea to change her mind, and hence let them off the hook, Jason returns and Medea sets in train the sequence of murders.

Euripides brings back the children at this juncture and the reason can only be to drill home the point about what is now at stake. By the end of the scene Jason has been lulled into believing that his pragmatism has converted Medea, and the Chorus have lost their chance to intervene. The Tutor, who is not privy to Medea's plot, returns alone and reveals that the princess has accepted the poisoned robe. The die is cast. But is it? Medea is doomed, but the Tutor has the children with him and a single word from the Chorus could still save them. The Chorus keep quiet. Medea offers up her long and heart-rending speech of farewell to her sons. She takes them into the palace and the paralysed Chorus can do no more than sing a song about the joys and sorrows of having a family. It is no use suggesting, as some have, that the Chorus fail to act because choruses do not initiate action or break their given word. In a number of plays, from Aeschylus onwards, if circumstances demand it, they do affect the plot. Here Euripides draws attention to a lack of *will* to act, and in this resides the play's most telling message.

The horror of the death of Jason's new bride and her father, as related by the Messenger, is only a prelude to Medea's murder of the children off-stage, while the Chorus outside listen to their screaming. Jason returns, discovers what has happened and batters at the doors to Medea's house. What confronts him is not the expected tragic tableau wheeled on at ground level, but an epiphany, with Medea transfigured as she appears aloft in a winged chariot with the children's corpses and justifies her actions in a manner that looks forward to Dionysos' final appearance in the *Bacchae*.

The parallel to the later play does not stop here. Medea is a creature of passion, a passion which is beyond the comprehension of anyone else in the play. The 'rational' characters try to make allowance for her foreign ways and are wary of her witchery, except when it is convenient. Like Dionysos in the *Bacchae*, or Artemis and Aphrodite in *Hippolytos*, Medea is a fact of life. Tangle with this sort of power and see what you get. Inevitably the play lends itself to being a platform for feminist opinion. Powerful enough at that level, it also makes a major contribution to Euripides' wider debate on human nature. He sets up a Greek Pinkerton and marries him to a hornet, not a butterfly. Loathe Jason as any audience must, the play has a deeper concern than watching a selfish pig get his come-uppance. Raw instinct, it tells us, and expedience are no match. Only by forcing the callous Jason to share her pain does Medea begin to make him realise what she is. The cool brutality of civilisation nurtures bloody destruction. There is the message, the implications of which every 'civilised' country in the world would be wise to heed.

The Phoenician Women

The story of Oedipus and his family is one that most of today's theatre-goers will feel they know. This puts them into a roughly similar position to the Athenian audience who first encountered *The Phoenician Women*. A modern audience will soon discover that they too are at the mercy of Euripides, who clearly did not believe that the last word had been said about that haunted king and his mother/wife.

By the time that Euripides presented *The Phoenician Women*, probably at the Great Dionysia of 409 BC, Aeschylus' *Seven Against Thebes* (467 BC) and two of Sophocles' Theban plays, *Antigone* (442 or 441 BC) and *Oedipus Tyrannus*, which is also known as *Oedipus Rex* or *Oedipus the King* (?429 BC), had become 'classics', definitive versions to which all others would be referred. The Sophocles pair deal, in reverse chronological order, with events before and after those of *The Phoenician Women*. The Aeschylus play covers the same ground. Euripides might have seen the original *Seven Against Thebes* as a boy of about thirteen. He would almost certainly have been part of the first audience for *Antigone* and *Oedipus Tyrannus*. As the originality of Euripides gives his play its dramatic impetus, it is worth pointing initially to how he varied his inherited plot.

According to Sophocles, by the time Oedipus finally discovers that he has fulfilled the oracle which forecast that he would murder his father and marry his mother, Jocasta has already realised the truth and departed the scene to commit suicide. Oedipus finds her hanging and puts out his eyes. Creon assumes sole kingship and accedes to Oedipus' request that he be sent away from Thebes. There the *Oedipus Tyrannus* ends. Sophocles' *Oedipus at Colonus*, not yet written in 409 BC, covers Oedipus' arrival at Colonus, his last resting-place, and the remaining hours of his life. *Antigone*, the earliest performed, takes up the story again in Thebes, a city preserved from the horrors of civil war only by the death in single combat of Oedipus' sons, Eteocles and Polyneices, but torn apart once more by Creon's refusal to permit the burial of Polyneices and Antigone's defiant stand against him. Aeschylus' *Seven Against Thebes* features Eteocles and contains no other members of the family except Antigone and Ismene, who enter late to lament their brothers in a sequence which some modern critics consider spurious.

All this needs emphasising because *The Phoenician Women* has the feel – and by no means for the first time in Euripides – of being less an alternative view of the myth than a positive riposte to the work of the previous dramatists. He opens with a very much alive Jocasta – the first surprise – who gives her version of the past in a prologue speech to the audience. Here there are some minor variations from Sophocles relating to Oedipus' birth and upbringing, and a major one when it transpires that Oedipus killed Laius on the way *to* Delphi and then returned home to Corinth without ever receiving Apollo's oracle that he would kill his father and marry his mother. Whatever degree of blame may be attached to Oedipus by Sophocles, in Euripides he is absolved from any charge of having flouted Apollo's word.

When Oedipus discovered the truth about his marriage to his own mother, Jocasta continues, and his dual relationship with his four children, Eteocles, Polyneices, Antigone and Ismene, he blinded himself and was shut away by his sons. He is not now in exile, but living in the palace. Angry and humiliated, he has invoked a powerful curse on his sons and it is around this curse, that they should 'inherit from me the sword and the sword's edge', that the play revolves. Eteocles and Polyneices then made a deal that they should rule year and year about. When Eteocles' term as King of Thebes was complete, he refused to hand over the throne. Polyneices has responded by raising an army to attack his native city. Here is another divergence from familiar Sophocles, though this time from the *Oedipus at Colonus*, still no more than a twinkle in the old man's eye. In Sophocles Polyneices is the elder brother, driven from Thebes by the younger Eteocles with whom no power-sharing deal has been struck. In *Seven Against Thebes* the brothers could well be twins, and neither lays claim to Thebes as his birthright. In Euripides, it is Eteocles who is the elder, though he declines to use this to justify his attitudes, but Polyneices who is their mother's undoubted favourite.

Aeschylus offers the point of view only of Eteocles in *Seven Against Thebes*, Sophocles that of Polyneices in *Oedipus at Colonus*, in a scene where he visits his father seeking a blessing for his attack on Thebes, a blessing which he singularly fails to get. Euripides tackles the issue with a head-on clash between the brothers, in a scene where the playwright seems to invite the audience to make a straight comparison with Aeschylus on the assumption that they will be familiar with the earlier play. One honour accorded to Aeschylus after his death, and apparently to no one else during the fifth century BC, was that his plays could be offered in revival as a festival entry. *Seven Against Thebes* was after all one of the plays that the 'dead' Aeschylus, as a character in Aristophanes' *Frogs*, chose to quote in support of his case for being considered premier playwright in Hades. And *Frogs* was performed only four years after *The Phoenician Women*.

This *ad hominem* approach of Euripides is in evidence on a number of occasions. The most celebrated is after Creon has suggested that the defence of the city be entrusted to a champion at each of the seven gates. In Aeschylus, single combat is proposed and each of the enemy champions is named and described so that Eteocles may find a suitable opponent, up to the final gate which Polyneices will attack with only Eteocles left to confront him. This selection of warriors occupies a full third of *Seven Against Thebes*, as the tension mounts, Eteocles apparently unaware that his brother is one of the seven. Euripides has no time for such pussy-footing. 'I'll go round our seven gates, as you suggest,' he declares, 'and set a chosen man at each . . . I'll name them later – now would be wasting time.' Then for good measure he adds, 'But the one they set against me, god willing, will be my brother' (748–751). The dig at Aeschylus is combined with a clear indication that the brothers have all along been spoiling for a fight.

The novelty of Euripides' approach is in the attention he draws to the dramatic method of his predecessor in order to deride it. Perhaps 'deride' is the wrong word. Parody would be more appropriate, and this is no isolated example. In *Elektra*, Euripides' heroine is dismissive about the tokens by which brother and sister recognise one another in Aeschylus' parallel play, *The Libation-Bearers*. The echo is undeniable. In *Orestes*, Euripides points to the inconvenience of a singing and dancing chorus turning up when Elektra has just succeeded in lulling her exhausted brother to sleep. Later in the same play a Messenger speech is delivered by a foreign slave in fractured Greek. Certainly this is closer to a parody of existing conventions than simply mockery of them. Perhaps even 'parody' underestimates the full purpose of Euripides. He is writing for a theatre tradition more than a hundred years old and for an audience whose increasing sophistication may be assumed from the sheer number of plays they may have witnessed, but who seemed to have grown morally and intellectually lazy. This is the method of an Ibsen or a Brecht, constantly challenging, often through the sly joke.

So much emphasis on the difference between this version of the story and others is more than academic juggling. Euripides inherited a theatre of stern, if not inflexible, conventions. He seems to have seen it as his duty, artistically, perhaps socially and politically too, to confront his audience with what they had come to take for granted and to surprise them from their complacency. Refinements to the plot, subtlety of motivation and frankness of expression all serve this end. *Seven Against Thebes* was the model for the patriotic statement on stage, combining a call for fortitude in the face of a common enemy with a warning against civic disruption. With the same story Euripides offered to a shattered and war-torn populace the complete destruction of a self-cursed family as an image of their own impending annihilation.

The Phoenician Women has always had its detractors, dismayed by, or at best apologetic about, its structure. Certainly there is a parade of incidents rather than an integrated plot: Antigone and the Tutor reviewing the army; Polyneices arguing his case with Eteocles; Teiresias forecasting disaster unless Creon's son is sacrificed; a first Messenger informing Jocasta and Antigone of Menoeceus' death; a second telling Creon of the deaths on the battlefield; Antigone's defiance of Creon; and finally Oedipus alone amidst the carnage. H.D.F. Kitto, whose defence of the play was more spirited than most, suggested that it should be regarded as a 'pageant' or as 'very good cinema'. Defensive as this might sound, it does serve to give licence to a consideration of the play in its own terms rather than in those of Aristotle, or of any later critic who has seen fit to ascribe to Greek tragedy a rigid formula.

As it is written, and still more as it is performed, there is a perfectly good unifying factor that demolishes most of the complaints against the play's episodic nature. Jocasta, Antigone, Polyneices, Eteocles, Creon and Menoeceus are all part of one family:

> One blood, one race,
> Descended all
> From the horn'd moon-maiden, Io,
> We share one agony.
>
> (*ll.* 247–249)

This is a cursed house and the curse reaches into every last corner, to be shared, like it or not, by all who suffer the kinship. The initial curse was laid on Oedipus before he was born, an Oedipus blameless for the acts of parricide and incest, but responsible for reinforcing the gods' curse upon the heads of his sons with his own. Here is the biggest cast in any Greek tragedy and apart from a couple of messengers, a tutor and a prophet, they are all related to Oedipus. Not even the Chorus are exempt, tied, however tenuously, by blood to the house and caught up in the war by pure mischance. Oedipus is held back as a character until his nephew, his sons, and his mother/wife are all dead. Only then does the blind man enter to preside over the final scenes. Without even the consolation of exhausted quiet which marks the aftermath of many a tragedy, he has to listen to Creon threatening the life of his daughter who has pledged to bury Polyneices' body, while three other corpses lie at his feet. Antigone's reprieve, to escort her father into exile, is the prelude to the most pathetic of scenes, with Oedipus feeling for the faces of first Jocasta then his sons, for whose death he has been at least partly responsible.

Sophocles constructed a concentrated vision that has made of Oedipus a universal icon. To that extent *The Phoenician Women* will always suffer by comparison with *Oedipus Tyrannus*. With his opening prospect of a city under plague, Sophocles reflects the first years of the Peloponnesian War, for *Oedipus Tyrannus* was close in time to *Medea*. Sophocles shows something innately heroic in Oedipus' single-minded search for himself, something positive, optimistic even, despite the appalling nature of the denouement. Euripides' *The Phoenician Women* is from twenty years later, when any hope of an Athenian victory has been dissipated; when the curses of atrocity, deprivation and defeat have left no family in the land untouched; and when disaster can be laid at the door of human folly rather than divine displeasure. For Sophocles' Oedipus, exile and poverty await, but there will be a triumphant end, as he is summoned by the gods to transfiguration. If such an outcome is at the end of the road for Euripides' Oedipus, *The Phoenician Women* gives no hint of it. Here is only the despair of a playwright whose unhappy departure from his native land for ever was but a couple of years away.

In 409 BC, when the play was probably first presented, Athens was in the unusual position of having won two naval victories within two years, but Euripides cannot have been alone in realising that Athens was losing the war. The level of specific allegory contained in *The Phoenician Women* must evade a modern audience, but the warning it contains is modern enough. Disaster, however distant, leaves no one untouched. None of us can escape the curses inflicted on us by past generations, neither innocent idealist nor cynical in-fighter. Worse, the misery is compounded by the curses we inflict. Euripides' picture is a bleak one, created out of bleak times. He is today's playwright, writing plays for today.

Bacchae

Greek tragedy is well endowed with people who inherit the fruits of their past actions. Jason initiated his own fate from the moment he first chose to use and abuse the love that Medea conceived for him. Oedipus was on a similar long fuse, one not primed by him, but ignited by the curse he called down on his sons. The *Bacchae* too concerns the legacy of the past and takes strands from both *Medea* and *The Phoenician Women*. Dionysos is an outsider, as is Medea, and he reacts to rejection with similar appalling results. He is at the same time a member of the ruling house of Thebes. His determination to reinstate himself leaves none of the rest of them untouched.

In each of the three plays in this volume the past catches up with the protagonists and the disintegration of family that results can all too easily appear as an image of the disintegration of society itself. *Medea* and *The Phoenician Women* both work as parable plays whose mythical ethos is no more than the bare bones of a story which is universal in its implications. The *Bacchae* resembles them in this, but possesses in addition a quality of mystery, which makes it quite unlike any other Greek drama. It is a mystery rooted in the identity of Dionysos himself.

Dionysos was god of the vine and of vegetation. He was also the god associated with the natural cycle and the changing seasons, the sufferer who died and was reborn. In this he preceded the Olympians and outlived them. Few cultures are without him in one form or another. His influence is perennial. To the Athenians there was the more specific aspect of his character, summed up in the title of E.R. Dodds' classic study, *The Greeks and the Irrational*. Dionysos was the god of ecstasy – ecstasy as a term to be taken literally, a 'standing outside of oneself' – and the god of unreason. This is the Dionysos of the faith-healer and the trance-dancer, of all those supra-normal powers which Teiresias notes and which so aggravate Pentheus by being beyond his explanation. The Dionysos of the *Bacchae* has at his disposal the power to derange. In his prologue speech to the audience he informs them that he has driven the women of Thebes mad, so that they now wander in the mountains, unaware of what they are doing. Later in the play his power is seen at close quarters when he escapes from imprisonment and then bewilders Pentheus into dressing as a woman in order to view for himself the Bacchic rites. When Pentheus' mother Agauë returns to the stage brandishing his head, she is still under the influence of the god and has to be brought back to reality by her appalled father.

The play offers several puzzles, paradoxes even, but one feature is clear. Whether or not Pentheus, as King of Thebes, has any right to try to restore normality to a situation that appears out of control does not affect the nature of Dionysos' influence. Dionysos exists. Apollo, a god of reason and harmony, may represent a saner ideal, but the world is not notably sane and the Dionysiac can break out at any time.

This factor alone is worth holding to when tackling what has become a critical minefield. A bibliography on the *Bacchae* runs to several hundred books and articles, many of them concerned with promoting a case for either Dionysos or Pentheus as the party in the right. 'Pentheus', one argument runs, 'is the fascist dictator, wielding a blinkered authority and deserving anything that he gets.' 'Dionysos', the King's apologists will counter, 'is a petty and vindictive sadist whose vaunted freedom conceals a demoniac coldness.' It is doubtful whether either extreme offers a tenable interpretation of the piece as a whole. In pure dramatic terms there is limited mileage, as even Aeschylus discovered, in the struggle between saint and sinner. In the light of other Euripides plays, something more subtle should be expected.

Euripides' world is not one in which moral decisions are easy, and an audience's attitude to the protagonists may change as time passes. Sure of themselves, the characters compete to be thought sane, but sanity is not the perogative of those who claim it. For Euripides, moral certainty is linked to madness. When Dionysos gets to work on the self-righteous Pentheus, he uncovers and brings to the surface Dionysiac qualities within Pentheus, hitherto dormant. Pentheus' moralising masks a deeper prurience, a fascination with precisely those things he claims to deplore. 'One thing more,' says Dionysos, as Pentheus threatens to call out the troops against the women who have deserted Thebes to worship their god. 'You would like to watch them/Up there in the mountains, wouldn't you?'

'Watch them?' replies Pentheus. 'Why, yes' (*ll.* 809–811). And he is hooked.

If Pentheus is shown to be morally fallible, a contributor to his own destruction, the ambiguity of Dionysos' motivation is likewise thrown into relief. What emerges in the scene where he reveals himself at last as a god – during the major part of the play he is 'disguised as a man' – is his human as opposed to his godlike nature. Everything relates back to his mother's rejection by her family.

Dionysos' mother was Semele, one of four daughters of Kadmos, the others being Agauë, Ino and Autonoë. Seduced by Zeus, Semele became pregnant. Jealous Hera persuaded Semele to get Zeus to reveal himself to her in his proper form. She chose her moment to extract a promise on which Zeus could not renege and was burnt to a cinder for her pains. What Hera had neglected to tell her was that Zeus' real nature was a lightning-bolt. In the nick of time, though not for Semele, Zeus rescued the embryonic Dionysos and sewed him up in his thigh, from where in due course he was born. This unorthodox entry into the world is more bizarre than most births even in myth. Euripides is at some pains, perhaps with tongue in cheek, to offer, in the mouth of Teiresias, the contemporary Athenian sceptic's account of such a tale. But this was the story, and it is this divine aspect of

Dionysos that Semele's sisters have denied. At the same time
there is the human dimension. Whatever the full significance of
the god's arrival in Thebes and his power to scramble the wits of
his opponents, at the heart of the play there is, as in *Medea* and
especially *The Phoenician Women*, a thoroughly domestic squab-
ble, which provokes Dionysos' act of vengeance upon Kadmos
and the rest of his kin.

The human part of Dionysos resents his exclusion from the
family. Whatever the faults of Pentheus, and whether they should
be attributed to youthful inexperience or a rather nasty nature,
the warmth of feeling between him and his grandfather is
undeniable. Pentheus castigates the prophet Teiresias as much
for making his grandfather look a fool as for pursuing the
Dionysiac cause. Kadmos has looked to Pentheus for protection
ever since he abdicated in his favour. One of the most moving
reversals in the play sees the old man restored to dignity as he
returns with his beloved grandson's remains to face his gleeful
daughter with the truth that the 'lion's head' she is brandishing is
not what she thinks.

A break in the manuscript has robbed us of the exact words
with which Dionysos returns to the scene, no longer *incognito*, but
recognisable as the god. High above the action he reviews the
ruins of the family to which he claims kinship. The amorality of
the god part has disqualified him from the company of the family
his human part seems to crave. The exchange between his
grandfather and the god offers one of the play's most powerful
moments:

KADMOS. We admit that we were wrong.

DIONYSOS. Too late. You acknowledge me far too late.

KADMOS. We know that, but you are too severe.

DIONYSOS. You offended me, me a god.

KADMOS. A god should not show passion like a man.

(*ll.* 1343–1348)

The response sets even Dionysos back on his heels and gives
emphasis to the sheer humanity of Euripides' approach to the
story.

As in *The Phoenician Women*, it is the Chorus who give this play

xxxiii

its title. In the earlier piece this takes some explaining, but in the *Bacchae* there is no difficulty. Tempting as some commentators have found it to treat this emphasis on the Chorus as a return to the Aeschylean pattern of the *Suppliants* or *Eumenides*, nothing else in Euripides suggests a playwright falling back on old devices. Quite the reverse. This chorus shows a stylistic advance on any other extant play, echoing the unseen chorus up in the hills and making the invisible visible. These Bacchants embody the Dionysiac religion itself in its total nature – peaceful, seductive, wilful, dangerous, malevolent, possessed. They are acolytes of the god, but simultaneously a corporate embodiment of his power. Their theatrical potential is as powerful as anything in the Greek theatre. Once this potential has been appreciated, many of the play's production problems evaporate. Even the earthquake which destroys Pentheus' palace, a destruction to which the King makes no subsequent reference, is simply a demonstration of Dionysos' power seen through the eyes of his attendant Chorus.

As is clear from other plays, Euripides works with and around the mechanics of his theatre. In other tragedies, choruses of assorted slaves, suppliants and citizenry are variously excused, or tolerated, as part of an inherited dramatic structure. These Asian Bacchanals marry their true identity to their figurative being. Pentheus threatens them with prison as undesirable aliens for rampaging about in front of his palace, but the threat they pose as a living extension of Dionysos himself is one to which he is blind. Once only, at the entrance of Agauë, do they suggest that they could feel pity and might perhaps, as human beings, dissociate themselves from Dionysos' vengeance. He is not present at the time and his timely reappearance restores their allegiance. An audience, initially sympathetic to the Dionysos oppressed by his regimented cousin and in harmony with the gentler sentiments of the Chorus, will find themselves by the end no longer able to subscribe to the mayhem the god has initiated. Echoes from the *Medea* are irresistible.

Perhaps all this seems too much like prescribing a 'correct' view, undesirable with a play of such breadth and complexity. There can never be a definitive *Bacchae*. There are, though, undeniable turning-points in the text, as there are in *Medea* and *The Phoenician Women*, where the audience are forced to reappraise. Euripides is crafty at engineering turns of event which make things appear in a new light. Pentheus versus Dionysos may be a simple collision between temporal and spiritual priorities. That collision can provide a starting point for a thematic dissection of the *Bacchae*, but it is no more than a starting point for a play whose richness is a constant source of wonder.

The *Bacchae*, like most great plays, is a number of things at once and intertwines ideas at differing levels of perception, each or any of which may dominate in different productions or for different members of a single audience. It is a play in which illusion wrestles with reality, a play about the quality of religious experience, about maleness and femaleness and the nature of sexuality, a black comedy, a family saga, a revenge tragedy, a threat to society, a plea for compassion. In other words it is one of that small and select band of plays against which all the rest, and not only from the Greek repertoire, must be judged. A formidable intellectual challenge, its substance is the demolition of intellect, argument and reason in the face of a power beyond analysis. That power is at least in part the power of the theatre itself where Dionysos is truly a god, able to make the scalp creep and the throat tighten. The *Bacchae* is Euripides' tribute to theatre.

J. Michael Walton

The line-numbering alongside the texts relates to the Greek original rather than the English translations.

Transliteration of Greek words, and, in particular, proper nouns, into English presents problems of consistency. In the previous edition of this volume, Medea *and* The Phoenician Women *followed different conventions from* Bacchae, *which, apart from the play's title, retains a Greek kappa (k) and omikron (o) in proper names. The new translation of* Medea *included here follows the Anglicisation of the first translation. Elsewhere, as with the names of the Greek playwrights, the guideline has been common usage.*

MEDEA

Translated by J. Michael Walton

Characters

NURSE *of Medea's children*
TWO SONS *of Medea and Jason (non-speaking)*
TUTOR
MEDEA
CHORUS OF LOCAL WOMEN
CREON, *King of Corinth*
JASON
AEGEUS, *King of Athens*
MESSENGER

Note. Off-stage speeches (Medea and children) were transmitted phonetically from the Greek in the first production. A transliteration is included in this version.

Corinth. Outside the house of Jason. Enter the NURSE.

NURSE. If only. If only the good ship *Argo*
  Had never negotiated the misty cliffs,
  Never beached at Colchis. If only.
  If only no forester had ever chopped the wood,
  No carpenter fashioned oars,
  For all those fine young men
  Whom Pelias sent to find the Golden Fleece.
  Then Medea, my mistress, would never have sailed for Iolcos,
  Besotted with her Jason.
  Never have persuaded those daughters of Pelias   10
  To kill their father. Nor had to flee here,
  To Corinth with her man and with their children.
  Oh, people liked her. Exile was bearable.
  And Jason. She did everything for Jason.
  The strongest fortress you can find,
  A woman and a man in partnership.
  Till now.

  Now love's betrayed, corrupted, turned to hate.
  Jason, the traitor, is leaving them, wife and family,
  To bed down with a princess, Creusa, Creon's child.
  A proper marriage.
  So Medea, poor Medea, is cast aside   20
  She curses him, calling on the vows they made,
  Imploring the gods to see his perfidy.
  She won't eat. Just lies there suffering.
  She can't stop crying.
  From the moment she heard how he'd betrayed her,
  She hasn't as much as raised her head.
  Her friends might as well talk to a stone or to the sea
  As expect her to listen to them.
  Just, now and then, a twist of the head   30
  Recalling the father she loved, her country,
  The home she gave up.

5

All for this man who's now had enough of her.
She knows now what it means to leave home.
Anywhere else you're a foreigner,
The chidren are no consolation. She can't look at them.
God knows what she may do next.
Suffering like that. I know her but she frightens me:

40   In case she sharpens a knife for her own heart,
Creeping silently through the house to her bed,
Or tries to kill the king, or the new bridegroom,
Provoking some irreparable disaster.
She's an odd one.
You'd be a fool to cross her lightly.

Enter the CHILDREN.

There are the children. They've been playing ball.
A mother's problems hardly trouble children.
Young hearts can't concentrate on grief.

Enter the TUTOR.

TUTOR. You silly old woman. You're just a piece of property.

50   What do you think you're doing out here,
Telling the world your troubles?
Medea needs you, doesn't she? In there.

NURSE. And you're a silly old man.
You may be the children's guardian
But aren't decent servants meant to feel anything
When disaster strikes the household?
All this. It's so upsetting.
I had to talk to someone about poor Medea,
Even if it's just the earth and the sky.

60 TUTOR. Has she stopped then? Stopped crying?

NURSE. You'd be lucky. Hardly started yet.

TUTOR. Daft. I shouldn't call her that, I know,
But she doesn't know the half of it.

NURSE. What are you on about, you old fool? Out with it.

TUTOR. Nothing. Nothing. I shouldn't have spoken.

NURSE. I'm not having this. We're both slaves, you know.
I'm not going to tell anybody, if I don't have to.

TUTOR. Well, I was pretending not to listen,
But I did hear someone say – down by the fountain

6

Where the old gaffers play dominoes –
That Creon means to send them packing, 70
Mother and children, away from Corinth.
That's what someone said but who can tell?
You know how these stories get about.
I just hope this one's wrong.
NURSE. What about Jason? He may have his differences with
Medea
But he's not going to let the boys suffer, is he?
TUTOR. You know what they say. New shoes run quicker than old.
But there's not many will stick up for him round here.
NURSE. That's us done for too, you realise.
A new problem to take on board, before we've unloaded the
last.
TUTOR. Hey. Listen, now. Not a peep out of you. 80
Not a word to the mistress. Understood?
NURSE. Poor boys. Did you hear that? That father of yours . . .
What a bastard. He may be my master
But not even a friend could defend him. He's rotten.
TUTOR. Who isn't? Where've you been all your life?
Everyone's interested in number one.
You'll find the odd just man, but few and far between.
Children can't compete with a new girlfriend.
NURSE. There now, boys. Don't you fret. In you go.
Just keep them out of the way, will you? 90
Don't let them go near their mother in this mood.
I didn't like the way she glared at them.
She looked dangerous. And I know her.
This mood's explosive. Someone's going to suffer.
Let's hope it's an enemy not a friend.
MEDEA (off). No! No! No!
Let me die.
[iô
dustanos egô melea te ponôn
iô, moi moi, pôs an oloiman?]
NURSE. Hear that, children?
Your mother's in trouble.
She's upset. Angry. Off you go.

100 Indoors. Quickly.
And don't let her set eyes on you.
In you go. Careful now.
There's a wildness there,
Something primitive,
Primitive and wilful.
Quickly. Indoors.
In a proud spirit
A distant cloud of grief
Can grow into a torrent.
What next?
Mercurial.
Unpredictable.
110 How will such a spirit react?
MEDEA (*off*). Pain.
Hate.
Cursed womb.
Accursed children
From such a father.
[*aiai,*
epathon tlamôn epathon megalôn
axi' odurmôn. ô kataratoi
paides oloisthe stugeras matros
sun patri, kai pas domos erroi.]
Enter the CHORUS.
NURSE. Poor things. No!
Why blame the children for the father's sin?
Why hate them?
Children, I fear for you.
The temper of the tyrant
Can be a fearful thing.
120 A habit of power
Condones viciousness.
Better the quiet life.
I'll settle for mediocrity
With peace of mind,
Moderation the watchword.
Ambition brings its own return,

8

God's envy. Further to fall. 130
CHORUS. I heard her voice.
   I heard her crying, poor foreign queen.
   MEDEA, off, sound of weeping.
CHORUS. There. Again.
   Old woman, tell me,
   I heard through the door
   That awful sound of sorrow.
   Such misery strikes to the heart.
   This has been a good house.
NURSE. House. A house but no longer a home.
   All gone.
   The man aspires to a bed in the palace. 140
   So she lives out her life in her room,
   Inconsolable.
MEDEA (*off*). A lightning bolt through the brain.
   I'd welcome that.
   What possible reason for living?
   Please death, please free me from this life,
   Become intolerable.
   [*aiai*
   dia mou kephalas phlox ourania
   baié; ti de moi zén eti kerdos?
   Pheu, pheu! thanatô katalusaiman
   biotan stugeran prolipousa.]
CHORUS. Lord of the earth and lord of light,
   Did you hear that?
   She sounds distraught. 150
   Why seek to welcome death,
   Poor woman? It hurries quick enough.
   Don't spur it on.
   Your husband's deserted you.
   For someone else's bed.
   That's not the end of the world.
   God will work it out.
   You mustn't take so hard the loss of a husband.
MEDEA (*off*). Goddess of justice, goddess of childbirth, 160
   Look down on me and my pain.

9

We made promises.
Now he's broken his.
I want her dead.
I want the pair of them obliterated,
Burnt to death in their own home,
Who dared to do me damage.
Oh my father! Oh my home that I abandoned!
Forgive me for the brother that I killed.
*[Ô megala Themi kai potni' Artemi,
leusseth' ha paschô, megalois horkois
endésamana ton katararaton
posin? Hon pot' egô numphan t'esidoim'
autois melathrois diaknaiomenous,
hoi' eme prosthen tolmôs adikein.
ô pater, ô polis, hôn apanasthên
aischrôs ton emon kteinasa kasin.]*

NURSE. Do you hear that?
    She calls on Zeus and Themis,
170   The gods who secure promises.
    She'll not take this lying down.
CHORUS. Perhaps she might come out.
    And then, perhaps, she'd listen
    To what we have to say,
    We could suggest that she control
    That temper of hers.
    I can always advise a friend, I hope.
180   Go on into the house
    And bring her out.
    Tell her we're all friends here.
    Hurry, before she does something stupid.
    This sort of grieving gets out of control.
NURSE. I doubt if I can persuade her,
    But I'll try, if it will make you happy.
    She's like a wild animal with the servants,
    A lioness, protecting her cubs,
    When anyone as much as speaks to her.
190   Those old bards missed the point,
    Celebrating the joyful things in life

10

In comfort at feasts and festivals.
Instead they should have tried
To soothe away life's misery and pain,
For families racked by misfortune or by death.
Music should offer consolation.   200
What does it do? Protects the well-fed
By papering over the cracks.
Exit NURSE.

CHORUS. I heard her.
I heard that ecstasy of grieving
Directed at the traitor to her bed.
She calls on the gods to avenge her wrongs,
Protectors of the promise
Which brought her over the salt and murky sea   210
Here to Greece where that oath was broken.
Enter MEDEA.

MEDEA. There now. I've come outside.
I wouldn't want to be reproached, my Corinthian friends,
For being high and mighty. Indoors and aloof.
If you like a quiet life they'll call you antisocial.
But when were first impressions reliable?
One man will hate another for no reason
The moment he claps eyes on him.   220
A gut reaction but where's the justice in that?
If you're a foreigner, well, it's best to conform.
Even a citizen can't make the rules
Simply to suit himself. That would be bad manners.
But I . . . I was not expecting this.
It pierces me to the soul.
You are my friends. I've lost the will to live.
My life was centred on one man, my husband.
A hollow man.
Poor women.   230
No living, breathing creature feels as we do.
We want a husband? It's an auction
Where we pay to give away our bodies.
That's not the half of it. A good man or a bad?
By the time you find that out it's too late.

11

Divorce for a woman means disgrace.
And once she's married, there's no saying 'no'.
It's her who has to change the patterns of her life.
You'd need to be clairvoyant
240   To know how to behave in bed.
If you do strike lucky
And this husband turns out bearable,
Submits gracefully, then fine. Congratulations.
If not, you might as well be dead.
When a man starts to get bored at home
He can visit a friend, some kindred spirit,
Look for consolation elsewhere.
We have a single focus, him.
You've a nice, easy life, that's what they say,
Safe at home when they're off fighting.
Good thinking, that is, isn't it?
250   I'd fight three wars rather than give birth once.
Our situations are different, of course.
This is your city. Your father's house was here.
Life at its best, with your friends around you.
But I'm alone, stateless, abused
By a husband like something picked up abroad.
No mother. No brother. No relation
To turn to in a time of trouble.
That's why I'd like to ask for your support.
260   If I hit upon some means, some stratagem,
To pay my husband back for what he's done,
The bride and giver of the bride he means to marry,
Say nothing.
A woman's always full of fears, of course,
Petrified by the mere sight of steel.
But scorn her, cross her in love,
And savour the colour of her vengeance.
CHORUS. Of course. Pay him back, Medea.
That's only fair. You suffer. Why shouldn't you?
Look out – Creon. Here comes the king.
270   Some new development.
Enter CREON.

12

CREON. I know that sullen look directed at your husband.
    I want you out of here, Medea,
    Out of this country and those boys with you.
    And I want it now. I've made a decision.
    I'm not returning home until you've gone.
MEDEA. I'm helpless. What do you expect me to do?
    Everyone against me. No refuge.
    Creon, I have done nothing.   280
    Why are you banishing me?
CREON. Because you frighten me.
    I'll not mince words. I'm frightened
    You might devise some mischief against my daughter.
    And do you know why I'm frightened?
    Because you're clever. And you're capable of anything.
    You've been kicked out of your husband's bed
    And you're angry. I've heard your threats –
    They told me – against the bride, the groom,
    All of us. So I'm taking no chances.   290
    Rather your hatred now than regret later.
MEDEA. Clever? I've been called that before, Creon.
    I've a reputation, haven't I, for causing trouble?
    No man in his right mind
    Should teach his children to be clever.
    No point in being cleverer than the next man.
    People don't like it. They get jealous.
    Try new ideas on idiots and they'll hate you.
    So, what's the point?
    Become more famous than the sages,   300
    They'll hate you more than ever.
    I do speak from experience here.
    Yes, I'm called clever. As an insult,
    Meaning envied, or sullen, or peculiar,
    Or solitary. Well, I'm not that clever.
    So you're afraid of me, Creon.
    What am I going to do that's so terrible?
    I can't do much to damage a king.
    And why harm you? Did you harm me?
    You gave your daughter to the man of your choice.   310

13

True I hate my husband, but you did something sensible.
I don't grudge you your prosperity.
As for their marriage – good luck to it.
Just let me stay. I'm the victim here,
But you can't argue with power. I'll keep quiet.
CREON. It all sounds very docile,
But what's going on inside that head of yours?
Something nasty. I trust you less than ever.
You know where you are with a hothead, woman or man.
320   They're easier to fathom than the silent types.
Go. Now. Without another word.
It's decided. You're a baleful influence here.
No trick you pull can change that.
MEDEA. Please. I beseech you. In your daughter's name.
CREON. Don't waste your breath.
MEDEA. I'm begging you.
CREON. My family come first.
MEDEA. My country! My country!
CREON. *My* country! *My* country and *my* family.
330   MEDEA. Oh, the curse that is love.
CREON. Depending on the circumstance.
MEDEA. The cause. For god's sake remember the cause of this.
CREON. Take yourself off. You're nothing but trouble.
MEDEA. Trouble, yes. Trouble and more trouble.
CREON. Do you want the servants to throw you out?
MEDEA. Please, Creon!
CREON. You're making a scene.
MEDEA. I'll go. I'll go. Just one thing. Please.
CREON. Then go. Why make such a fuss about it?
340   MEDEA. One day. Let me stay one more day.
I need time to think about banishment.
The children. To make provision for the children,
Since their father can't be bothered,
Take pity on them. You're a father yourself.
You must show some humanity.
I'm not worried about myself.
Exile is exile but for them it's a disaster.
CREON. I'm not a bully. It's not in my nature.

14

And I paid for it in the past.
This time too, probably.   350
Yes. All right. But I give you fair warning –
If the light of tomorrow's dawn finds your sons
Or you within our borders, it's death.
That's final. Stay a last day if you must.
You can't get up to much mischief in one day.
Exit CREON.
CHORUS. Poor woman.
    Trouble on top of trouble.
    Where are you to turn?
    Where do you look for protection?
    For a welcome or a home?   360
    That's where some god has left you,
    Medea, rudderless in a storm.
MEDEA. Everything against me. So be it.
    We're not finished yet. Oh no.
    A gruesome coupling awaits this bridal pair.
    A sour wedding breakfast for the guests.
    I'd not suck up to him, unless I needed to,
    For what I'm planning. Not a word, not a touch.
    You'll see that, I'm sure.   370
    The fool!
    When all my plans are hanging by a thread
    He offers me a day before my banishment,
    A day for me to transform the father and the daughter
    And my husband, three enemies into three corpses.
    A thousand deaths I have for them, dear friends.
    Where would be a good place to start?
    Fire the palace during the reception?
    Steal into the bridal suite
    And knife them *in flagrante*?   380
    One thing stops me. I might get caught.
    If they found me in the palace, red-handed,
    It's me who'd die, a mockery, a laughing-stock.
    Surest is safest. Stick to what you do best.
    Where's my expertise? In poison.
    A death sentence for them. But what about me?

15

What city will take me in, grant me asylum,
A home, security from avengers?
Nothing. Nowhere. Slowly now. Bide your time.
390   You want to get away with this.
Cunning. That's what these murders need.
And stealth. If I should fail . . . I'll take the sword
And turn it on myself. Suicide takes courage.
Now by Hecate, dark mistress whom I worship,
Partner-in-crime, co-conspirator,
Squatter in the corners of my mind, I swear,
No man damages me with impunity.
They'll rue this wedding-day I send them,
400   Rue their vows and rue my exile.
To the task, then.
Conjure, Medea, conjure all your craft.
Ooze into evil. Hold hard like a limpet.
Concentrate on grievance.
What jokes they'll make at the wedding,
Those Corinthian men. You can't have that,
You, a princess, a granddaughter of the Sun.
You have the knowledge, Medea.
After all, we women are good for nothing –
That's what they say – except causing trouble.
410 CHORUS. Rivers flow backwards,
What's right is wrong,
Corrupt counsel prevails:
There's no faith in god,
Because of men.
But times are changing:
Our deeds will be glorified.
An end to those slanders,
420   Celebration of women.

And all those old songs
With their stories of faithlessness,
Enough of them.
Apollo, god of music,
Gave his talent to men,
Excluding us women.

Had he not, I'd write songs,
New songs about heroines,
Not heroes but women.   430

But you left your home,
Passion in your heart,
Past the twin rocks
To a foreign country.
Suddenly waking
With your marriage in tatters,
Poor Medea, an exile,
Humiliated.

The sanction of a promise. Gone.
Shame at bad faith. Gone.
Nowhere in Greece,   440
Dispersed to the skies.
And for you, poor Medea,
No home to run to,
Your bed usurped,
Dispossessed.
Enter JASON.

JASON. If I've seen it once I've seen it a hundred times.
  Bad temper means trouble.
  You could have stayed here, you know,
  If you'd just knuckled down to do what you're told.
  Instead you've talked yourself into exile.   450
  So unnecessary. Well, it's no skin off my nose.
  You can tell the world what a swine Jason is.
  But all that against the royal family,
  You're lucky they only banished you.
  I've done everything I could, believe me.
  I never wanted you to have to leave.
  But denouncing them as tyrants,
  You must be off your head. Exile? Serve you right.
  Anyway, I don't bear grudges against loved ones.
  We need to think about your future. That's why I've come.   460
  We can't have you destitute, not with the children,
  It can be difficult, exile. All manner of problems.

17

So, hate me if you like, but I bear no grudge against you.
MEDEA. You bastard! Coward! Would there were words
To describe your cowardice.
You come here? You dare come here to me?
Perjured, lying bastard.
A real hero, aren't you, bold enough
470   To destroy your family and then face them out.
A legion of diseases prey on men,
But gall like yours is worse than a disease.
I'm glad you came, though. It gives me the pleasure
Of telling you what I think of you. Enjoy it.
Where to begin, that's the problem.
I saved your life. There's not a single Greek
Of those who crewed the *Argo* would deny that,
When you were sent off to tame fire-breathing bulls,
To yoke them and sow that deadly field.
480   Then there was the dragon, guardian of the Golden Fleece,
With all its massive coils, never sleeping.
Who killed it? I killed it and saved your reputation in the
                                                process.
It was me betrayed my father and my home
To land at Iolcos by Mount Pelion,
Fond as I was, fonder than was wise.
I caused the death of Pelias, a terrible death
At his children's hands, but all for you.
That's what I did for you and what's your rotten response?
Betrayal when you fancy some new wife.
490   I bore your children. Had I not,
You might have had excuse at least.
You broke your oath. Do you believe in gods,
You know those old-fashioned gods who used to be in control?
Or do you think men make the rules these days?
You broke your word to me.
By this right hand you used to hold,
Upon my knees I say 'You used me'
And I feel dirty from your touch.

Let's talk like friends, shall we,
500   Though I hardly expect fair treatment here.

Still. Your response should be revealing.
Where do you expect me to go? Back to my father's house?
The one I betrayed when I left with you?
To the daughters of Pelias, poor things, perhaps?
They'd have a welcome, I'm sure, for their father's killer.
That's it, you see. My friends are all enemies.
Because of all those dreadful things I did.
Because of all the dreadful things I did for you.
I do have a wonderful social position
Among Greek women. And a distinguished husband   510
Of course, an honourable man. But if I'm exiled,
Dear me, what then? And wander off with the children
All alone? People will talk. 'A new bridegroom, he may be,
But the children are begging, and the woman who made him.
You showed us, Zeus, how to tell gold from counterfeit.
Pity you didn't brand men to show the same.'
CHORUS. There's an anger that goes beyond all remedy   520
     When love turns to hate.
JASON. I'd best restrain myself, I think,
     And like a good helmsman on a ship
     Reef in the sail and run before the storm
     Of that unfettered tongue of yours.
     I have to say, as you claim a debt from me,
     That Aphrodite was my protectress on that voyage,
     The goddess, her alone and no one else.
     You're good with words, Medea. Perhaps it seems
     Unchivalrous to suggest that it was simply Love   530
     Whose arrows forced you to save my life.
     I don't want to make an issue of it.
     The assistance you gave was quite valuable.
     But you did get better than you gave,
     I think it's fair to say.
     To begin with, instead of that uncivilised place,
     You now live in Greece, a seat of justice
     And the rule of law instead of mindless violence.
     Everyone in Greece knows how clever you are.
     You're famous. If you'd still been living   540
     At the back of beyond, no one would have heard of you.

19

For my part, a house crammed full with gold,
Or the skill to sing and play like Orpheus,
Would have no meaning without the fame.
I've spoken so far of my own achievements
But you did initiate this debate.
As for my marriage, my royal marriage,
That was a clever decision, you must agree,
As well as a sensible one, the best thing really
550   For you and the boys. No, just wait a moment.
When I arrived here from Iolcos,
Weighed down by a series of disasters,
What greater ambition could I have had,
As an immigrant, than to marry the king's daughter?
It was not – and I know this is what upsets you –
That I'd stopped loving you and fancied some
New woman or wanted a bigger family.
The boys. They're fine. No complaints there.
But so we could live a respectable life –
That's what it all comes down to –
560   And never go short. Oh, I know what it's like
For a man who's poor. Friends shun him,
This way I could have another family,
As befits my station, and bring them up as brothers
For our boys, one big happy family.
You don't need any more children, but for me
More sons would be a benefit to the others. Do you see?
What's wrong with that? But for your sexual jealousy.
You women. You're fixated. You've convinced yourselves,
570   If you're happy in bed, nothing else matters.
If you're not, then everything's a disaster.
I wish there were some other way to father children.
No women. That would solve everything.
CHORUS. A pretty speech, Jason.
But hardly fair on your wife, I think.
MEDEA. I may be alone in this – I usually am.
580   But for me he's a double-dyed villain
Who cloaks his weasel-words in sophistry.
A tongue so glib and devious

Will know no boundaries. Too clever by half.
You can drop the rhetoric.
One word will be enough.
If any of this were true, you'd have talked to me
Before this marriage, not kept it all a secret.
JASON. And so I would but for your attitude.
Mention the word marriage and look at you.
You can't control your fury.   590
MEDEA. That's not it, is it? As time went on
You found it inconvenient to have a foreign wife.
JASON. You know perfectly well, it's nothing about the princess
That made me want a royal marriage.
I've told you already, I did it for you,
To protect you and to father some royal sons,
Half-brothers for ours. For security.
MEDEA. I can do without that sort of security.
You can't buy peace of mind.
JASON. That attitude will get you nowhere.   600
Learn to be pragmatic.
Ride you good luck. Don't disparage it.
MEDEA. Don't insult my intelligence.
My departure lets you off the hook.
JASON. Have it your own way. You've only yourself to blame.
MEDEA. My marriage? My betrayal? What am I meant to have
                                                        done?
JASON. Curse the royal family. That's what you have done.
MEDEA. Not only the royal family.
JASON. I can't talk to you.
If you want it, for the children or yourself,   610
If you want it, there's money.
Just say the word. I'm quite prepared
To help you get by. I've friends. Abroad.
It's a genuine offer. You'd be a fool to turn it down.
Control that temper of yours and you'll be fine.
MEDEA. References. To friends of yours.
No thank you. I won't be needing them.
'Beware Greeks . . .', as they say.
JASON. Oh for god's sake. I swear to you.

620   You, the boys, I only want to help.
       You don't know when you're well off, never have.
       That's your problem. You are so stubborn.
       All right. Spurn your friends. But on your head be it.
    MEDEA. Just go away, Jason! Your little bride's expecting you.
       You don't want to keep her waiting.
       Exit JASON.
       Go on. Go and get married. With luck,
       It won't be the wedding-day you have in mind.
    CHORUS. Passion. Too much passion.
       No merit in that,
       No reputation there.
630   Love, gentle love,
       Is a gift of the gods.
       I'll settle for that,
       With no searing, no poison,
       No obsession, no pain.

       Control. Moderation.
       I'll pray for them,
       I'll be comfortable with them.
       God preserve me
       From that madness,
640   The affliction that is sex,
       Without rhyme, without reason.
       Affection, but not passion.

       This is my home,
       My country, my place.
       May I never lose it,
       Never stray from security.
       Nothing worse, more pitiful.
       Rather death. Death rather,
650   Than a life with no country,
       No home. Nowhere.

       We know from experience.
       We see for ourselves,
       No city for you,
       No friend to take pity.

That's suffering at its worst.
God's curse on the man
Who closes his mind   660
To the helpless. I hate him.
Enter AEGEUS.
AEGEUS. Medea. It's good to see you.
   The warmest greetings I can offer to a friend.
MEDEA. And good to see you too, Aegeus.
   You're welcome. What are you doing here?
AEGEUS. On my way home from the oracle.
MEDEA. The oracle? What did you want at Delphi?
AEGEUS. I'm childless. I wanted advice.
MEDEA. No family? God, no family?   670
AEGEUS. No family, no. Just bad luck, I suppose.
MEDEA. You are married? It's not, well, you know . . .
AEGEUS. Yes. I am married. We are married.
MEDEA. So, what did the oracle say?
AEGEUS. Excellent advice. I'm not sure quite what it means.
MEDEA. Can you tell me? The oracle? Would it be allowed?
AEGEUS. Oh, yes. It needs someone clever. Someone like you.
MEDEA. So? What did he say?
AEGEUS. He said 'Free not the wineskin's dangling foot.'
MEDEA. Till what? Till when?   680
AEGEUS. Till I get back home.
MEDEA. Oh. So, what are you doing here?
AEGEUS. There's someone called Pittheus – king of Troezen.
MEDEA. A god-fearing man, they say.
AEGEUS. I thought I'd tell him. Tell him the oracle.
MEDEA. A good man. He'll sort it out for you.
AEGEUS. The best. We've fought together. Side by side.
MEDEA. Well, good luck. I hope it works.
AEGEUS. You look troubled, a bit out of sorts. Anything the
                                                           matter?
MEDEA. That husband of mine, Aegeus. What a swine.   690
AEGEUS. What do you mean? You're upset. I can see that.
MEDEA. He's wronged me and it's not my fault.
AEGEUS. Why, what on earth has he done? Tell me.
MEDEA. He's got himself a new wife.

23

AEGEUS. How dare he!
MEDEA. And I, his former lover, I'm humiliated.
AEGEUS. Did he fall in love with someone? Or fall out of love with
you?
MEDEA. He's in love, all right, and to hell with his family.
AEGEUS. Good riddance, if he's that bad.
700 MEDEA. It's the palace he's in love with.
AEGEUS. I don't quite follow. Who's her father?
MEDEA. Creon, the king. Creon.
AEGEUS. Now I see why you're upset.
MEDEA. I'm done for. They've exiled me.
AEGEUS. This is monstrous. Who has?
MEDEA. Creon has. He's thrown me out of Corinth.
AEGEUS. And Jason let him? That's unacceptable.
MEDEA. He says he fought it, but he's coping.
    But I beseech, I beg you
710   By your head and by your knees,
    Have pity. Pity me in my misery.
    Don't see me left destitute.
    Let me into your country and your home,
    And love and good fortune will solve your problem,
    Grant you children and peace at the last.
    You don't realise what a stroke of luck you've had.
    I can cure your childlessness.
    I can make you a father. I know the remedy.
AEGEUS. For several reasons, madam, I'm inclined
720   To grant you what you ask. For the gods,
    And for the children that you promise me,
    Without whom Aegeus' name dies with him.
    So be it. Come to Athens and in good faith
    I'll do my best to see that you're safe.
    One thing only, I'll not help you leave.
    But find your way to where I live
    And I can guarantee your safety.
    But you must secure your own departure.
730   I want no trouble with strangers.
MEDEA. Fine. I'd like you to swear to that.
AEGEUS. You don't trust me? What's the matter?

24

MEDEA. I do trust you. But I have enemies.
   Creon and the house of Pelias.
   An oath cements my sanctuary.
   Your unsupported word, friend as you are,
   Without divine sanction, could be vulnerable
   Faced with a proclamation. I am powerless.
   They have money and a kingdom.   740
AEGEUS. You're looking ahead. That's good.
   If this is what you want, very well.
   Safest for me too, I think,
   To have a pretext for your enemies.
   Better for you too. Name your gods.
MEDEA. Swear by Mother Earth and by the Sun,
   My grandfather, and the whole pantheon.
AEGEUS. What am I swearing to do? Tell me.
MEDEA. Swear you will never send me from your country.
   Swear, whatever enemy demands,   750
   While you live, you'll never give me up.
AEGEUS. I swear. By the Earth, by the Sun,
   By all the gods, I swear to do as you require.
MEDEA. That's good. On pain of what?
AEGEUS. Whatever perjurers suffer.
MEDEA. Goodbye then. Be happy. Everything's going to be fine.
   I'll make for your city as soon as I can.
   There's something I have to do first.
CHORUS. May Hermes, the escort, protect you, Aegeus,
   Heading for home and the heart's desire   760
   That your generous spirit deserves.
   Exit AEGEUS.
MEDEA. Now Zeus, now Justice, daughter of Zeus,
   Now light of the Sun, triumph, sisters,
   Triumph over the enemy. We're under way.
   Now we have the luxury of hope.
   An escape route. That was my weakness.
   Then who turns up? He does, my port in the storm.
   He's where I'll tie my tow-rope,   770
   Heading for a home in Athens.
   Let me explain all I have in mind,

Not the most cheerful of listening.
I will send a servant for Jason
And ask him to come to see me.
When he comes I will be very conciliatory,
Telling him how right he is, I now realise.
His royal marriage is a good thing all round,
Even if it means betraying me.

780 I'll ask for the children to remain here.
I don't want them left here, of course,
For my enemies to degrade,
But as instruments in killing the princess.
I'll send them with gifts,
Bridal gifts, to ask for an amnesty.
Gifts of a delicate dress and a gold tiara.
And if she puts them on, they'll kill her.
And they'll kill anyone who touches her,
Because I'll saturate my gifts with poison.

790 When that is done, it's done.
But what comes next, ah, there are the tears.
I have to kill the children. My children.
No one shall take them from me.
When Jason's world's destroyed,
Then I'll leave this land, depart,
Pursued by the most unnatural of crimes,
My murder of my children.
Sisters, I will not be mocked.
This has to happen. What is life for me?
No country. No home. No escape.

800 My fatal mistake was the day
I left my father's house, seduced by this Greek
And his fine words – god make him pay.
He'll never see alive the boys I bore,
Nor father a son on this brand-new wife
Condemned to die from my doctoring.
No weak little woman, here, no doormat.
Let nobody think it. Oh, no.
A good friend, but what an enemy.

810 Famous for it. That's Medea!

26

CHORUS. You've let me share your mind. I'm on your side.
    You know that. But there are laws. We're human.
    Medea, you can't do this.
MEDEA. There's no alternative. Say what you like.
    It's easy for you. What do you know of suffering?
CHORUS. Kill the boys? You'd bring yourself to do that?
MEDEA. He'll feel it.
CHORUS. And what about you? What does that make you?
MEDEA. What I am. Defeated. No point in your protesting.

                                          Nurse,

   Enter NURSE.
   Fetch Jason.   820
   You've always been someone I could trust.
   Tell no one. Nothing to anyone, if you care for me.
   No. Not that. As you are a woman.
   Exit NURSE.
CHORUS. Athenians, sons of Erechtheus,
   Children of the gods, are blessed.
   In a holy land, clothed in peace,
   Nourished by judgement.
   Such air they breathe   830
   That Harmonia, golden Harmonia,
   Chose Athens, so they say,
   As birthplace for the Muses.

   They tell too of Aphrodite,
   By the chuckling river Cephisus,
   A breeze on her breath,
   A soft caress, no more,
   With roses in her hair,   840
   Offering love to the land,
   Love, tempered by moderation,
   Twin virtue with modesty.

   A city like that,
   A city of sacred rivers,
   Protector of travellers,
   To welcome an unholy child-killer?   850
   Murder. Look at it.

27

Look at it. Murder of your children.
Think again, I beg you.
Not killing your own children.

Where do you find the resolve,
The cast of mind, of heart,
To raise a hand against children,
Your own children?

860   Can you stare with steely eye
At those boys, your boys,
On their knees for their lives,
And lift your bloody hand?

Enter JASON followed by the NURSE.

JASON. You wanted to see me? Here I am.
I'm aware what you think of me, but, give me credit,
If you've something new to say, I'll listen.

MEDEA. Oh Jason, I'm sorry. Forgive me
870   For what I said. I was angry –
You know me. We were in love once.
I'm so furious with myself.
'What a fool you are, Medea,' I tell myself,
'To get upset with those who want to help,
Fighting the authorities, never mind your husband
Who only wants to do what's best for you,
Marrying a princess so my boys can have some brothers.
Control that temper of yours. You don't know
When you're well off, that's your problem.
There's the children, of course, but we're friendless,
880   On our own, living here on charity.'
So. I realise what a fool I've been,
Getting all upset. No point, is there?
In fact I have to thank you.
You did the sensible thing. I've been silly.
I should have been offering advice,
Giving a hand, making the new bed,
Happy to be your new wife's chamber-maid.
But, that's women for you. You know what we're like.
890   Don't pay us back in our own kind. Please.
Don't pay back foolishness with foolishness.

28

I give in. I've been very stupid.
But I'm better now.
Children. Children. Come out here a moment.
Hurry. Out here. Your father's here.
Come and see your father. And say goodbye.
Enter CHILDREN with the TUTOR.
We have to go. But no hard feelings.
We've made peace, your father and I.
We're friends again. Take his hand, then.
And the future? Well, who knows?   900
I'd rather not think about it. Oh children,
Your whole lives stretching out before you . . .
I'm frightened. I can't stop crying today.
There now. Quarrel's over with your father.
I can't see. I'm crying again.
CHORUS. And so am I. And so am I.
Please god, let things get no worse than this.
JASON. That's my girl. I don't blame you.
A woman's likely to get a bit emotional
With her husband marrying again.   910
Now you're making sense. Better late than never
But you can see the way the wind blows.
This is a reasonable woman talking.
You see, boys? Your father's had his thinking cap on.
God willing, he's sorted out your future for you.
You'll turn out to be big men, I think,
As big as your brothers in Corinth.
You keep growing, eh? And leave the rest
To your dad and any friendly god.
Fine lads you'll be when you're grown,   920
I reckon, ready to sort out my enemies for me.
Medea. Medea, why the tears?
You look as though you've seen a ghost.
I thought what I said would please you.
MEDEA. Nothing. It's nothing. I worry about them.
JASON. Come on. Cheer up. It'll work out fine.
MEDEA. You're right. Of course, you're right.
Us women. Always something to cry about.

29

JASON. But why are you worried about them?

930 MEDEA. I'm their mother aren't I? You talked about their future.
I just felt an ache. About the future.
Well, that is part of it. Why I asked you to come.
Let me tell you the rest.
It suited Creon's purpose, so it would seem,
To exile me. And so it suits me too.
I wouldn't wish to be an embarrassment
To you or to the palace, who seem to find me a threat.
So I'll take myself off, away from this land.
But so that the boys may be brought up by you,

940 Please ask Creon not to banish them.

JASON. I don't hold out much hope but I'l try.

MEDEA. Then tell your wife. Tell your wife
To ask Creon not to banish them.

JASON. Very well. She'll agree to that.

MEDEA. She's a woman. She'll agree.
And I must do my part too.
I'll send her presents, a dress, finely woven,
And a gold coronet, gifts as beautiful

950 As any you ever saw. The boys will take them.
Fetch them, one of you. Quick as you can.
Exit one of the CHILDREN.
A thousand blessings she shall win
With a man like you for a husband,
And decked out in finery my grandfather,
The Sun himself, handed down.
Enter CHILD *with a box.*
Here we are. Now boys, you must deliver these
Wedding presents to the princess, personally,
Into her hands. Special gifts.

JASON. Expensive presents. You are an idiot, Medea.

960 They've plenty of dresses in the palace.
And gold. Keep them. Don't give them away.
She'll take more notice of what I tell her
Than of any presents, I'm sure of that.

MEDEA. Don't say that. Even a god likes a present.
Gold speaks louder than words – that's what they say –

30

Fortune favouring her, that's all.
She's young. She's a princess. To save my sons
From exile, never mind gold, I'd give my life.
Now listen, children. When you go into the grand house
Approach our young princess, my mistress,   970
And beg her, on your knees, not to banish you.
Give her the presents – most important that –
Into her hands. Give them to her yourselves.
Quick as you can. As soon as you've done it,
Come back here with good news for your mother.
Exeunt CHILDREN, TUTOR, NURSE and JASON.
CHORUS. Any hope that I cherished for the children's lives
Snuffed out. Infanticide's abroad.
The bride who says 'yes' to the gold-crusted crown,
Says 'yes' to her death throes.
She holds in her hands for her golden head   980
A fatal decoration.

So enchanting, so seductive, so divine.
And the dress, like the crown.
Just the things for a bride, Hell's bride.
She'll be caught in the trap,
Webbed in by the sticky strands of Death,
Clinging, inexorable.

And Jason, oh Jason, the ill-starred bridegroom,   990
Son-in-law elect
To the royal family, unwitting carrier
Of death to your children,
To your bride an agonising fate,
Jason, what a downfall.

And Medea, oh Medea, pity for you too,
Mother and killer-elect
Of your own children for vengeance.
All over a new wife
And a husband leaving against his oath   1000
For some new bed.
Enter TUTOR and CHILDREN.
TUTOR. Success, mistress. No exile for the boys.

31

The princess accepted the gifts
And has made peace with your children.
What's the matter?
Why are you looking like that?
It's good news isn't it? Why turn away?
You should be delighted. Isn't this what you wanted?
MEDEA. No, oh no.
TUTOR. This is a strange reaction. My news is good news.
MEDEA. No. No. No.
1010 TUTOR. What did I say? I thought the news was good.
MEDEA. Your news was news. Not your fault.
TUTOR. Then why are you looking like that? Why the tears?
MEDEA. 'The infernal machine', old man. I've set in train
   Something fearsome, I and the gods.
TUTOR. Don't worry. The children will fetch you home in time.
MEDEA. I'll fetch home others first.
TUTOR. You're not the only one to be parted from your children.
   You have to grin and bear it. People do.
MEDEA. Then so must I. Off you go indoors, now,
1020   And get the children ready for the day.
   Exit TUTOR.
   Oh my boys, my boys. This is your city,
   Your home where I must leave you motherless.
   Poor me.
   I leave for somewhere else, a refugee,
   Without the joy of watching you grow up,
   Of seeing your prosperity, wives, weddings,
   Wedding-torches, wedding-beds.
   Selfishness, I suppose. It seems so pointless.
   Why did I ever cherish you?
1030   Why bear you at all?
   Difficult labours. Painful births.
   You have these hopes – I did, poor fool that I was –
   Of growing old pampered,
   With loving care to help you from this life.
   It's everyone's ambition. All gone.
   A lovely dream. Without you
   I'll live out my time fretting, embittered.

You'll never set eyes on your mother,
Never again. You'll have moved on.
No, don't. Don't look at me like that. 1040
Is that a smile? Will you ever smile again?
What am I to do? They melt my heart.
Dear friends, when I look at their faces,
My willpower deserts me. I can't do it.
Change of plan. I'll take them away.
What point in wracking their father's heart
If I break my own twice over?
No. Never. Change of plan.
And yet . . . What's the matter with me?
They'd laugh at me, my enemies, for going soft. 1050
Coward. Coward, I must be strong.
No weakening. No relenting.
Children. Indoors.
Exeunt CHILDREN.
Now. Any of you who does not share my mind,
Go about your business. My hand will not weaken.
No. No, you can't. Medea, you can't go through with this.
You poor fool, let your children go.
They'll live on with you. Be happy.
No. Never. By all the hounds of hell,
I'll not hand over children of mine 1060
For my enemies to scorn and spit upon.
They have to die. And if that's going to happen,
I bore them so I have to do the killing.
All settled. There's no escape.
The coronet's on her head. The bride princess.
I know it. The dress is destroying her.
And I am starting on a terrible journey,
Terrible for my children too.
I have to speak to them.
Children, come here. Come here,
Re-enter CHILDREN.
Give me your hands. 1070
Beautiful hands. Lovely faces.
I love you. Wish you well. But not here.

Your father appropriated 'here'.
A kiss. A hug.
Such sweet breath children have. Soft skin.
Off you go now. Go away!
Exeunt CHILDREN.
I can't look at you and do this.
No. Passion drowns my judgement,
1080 Passion the destructive force.
CHORUS. A woman shouldn't probe
The fine subtleties of myth,
Or the struggle for survival.
But I have. Often.
We share a sense, we women,
To help us understand.
An instinct. Some of us.
Only a few, perhaps, but some,
Not incapable of reflection.

1090 And I say this. Those who miss out
On experience.
Who never have children,
They're the lucky ones.
They never know, the childless –
They never have the chance –
What a child may bring,
Joy or grief, grief or joy.
The childless never see
That first sweet enchantment
1100 Shrivel, with time, into despair.

How to bring them up.
How to have something to leave them.
Will they turn out frivolous?
Will they turn out decent?
There's no predicting; and no end to it.
But worst, the worst
Of any human experience.
You become prosperous: they grow –
Good children, fine young people –

34

And then some accident . . .   1110
Death steals them away,
Spirits them underground.
How does anyone survive that?
Why make yourself vulnerable,
Mortals to be toyed with by gods?
MEDEA. Sisters, I've lived a long time
  Under that sentence.
  Look. Someone coming.
  Jason's man, in a hurry, out of breath.
  Must be momentous news.   1120
  Enter MESSENGER.
MESSENGER. Terrible. Medea.
  You have done something terrible, unnatural.
  You have to go. Escape. Go.
  By ship. On land. Any way you can.
MEDEA. What on earth could require such a flight?
MESSENGER. The royal princess is dead.
  Creon too, victims of your venom.
MEDEA. Yes. I like the sound of this.
  You do me good. My friend for life.
MESSENGER. What are you saying? Woman, you're mad.
  You hear the royal house disintegrates   1130
  And you're pleased? Have you no fear?
MEDEA. I choose to see things in a different light.
  But, please, don't be in such a rush.
  Tell us about their deaths. And the more they suffered,
  I can assure you, my friend, the happier you'll make me.
MESSENGER. When the children, those two boys of yours,
  Arrived with their father at the palace,
  They found it all decorated for the wedding,
  And us servants, who used to take your side,
  We were delighted. Word had got around, you see,
  That you and your husband had been reconciled.   1140
  People shook the boys' hands or patted their golden hair.
  I was so excited I followed them to the women's rooms.
  The princess – she has our allegiance now, not you –
  She turned her gaze on Jason lovingly

35

Until she caught sight of the two children,
Then turned away and wouldn't look at them,
White as a sheet, furious to find them there.
1150 Your husband tried to placate her, saying,
'Don't be angry. Look. They only want to love you.
Your husband's friends must be your friends too.
They've brought presents. Accept them.
And ask your father to reprieve them. For me?'
The moment she saw the finery, she couldn't resist,
And gave in to all he asked.
Father and sons were barely out the door
Before she snatched the gorgeous dress and put it on,
1160 Then the gold coronet, checking in the mirror,
Giggling at the reflection of herself
As she arranged her curls round the tiara.
Then up she jumped from her dressing-table
And prinked around the room on her little white feet,
Glorying in her presents, again and again,
Posing, checking from head to heel.
Then, all of a sudden, something dreadful.
She changed colour, staggered,
Started to shiver, managed just
1170 To fall on the bed, not on the floor.
An old servant mumbled a prayer,
Assuming some god-frenzy or a fit.
But one look at her mouth –
Froth was bubbling from her lips,
Eyes rolling, colour drained.
No prayer then but a howl.
Someone ran for her father,
Someone else for the new husband,
1180 To tell them what was happening to the bride,
The corridors echoing with running feet.
For the time it takes a runner to complete a lap
She lay mute, poor woman,
Then started up, eyes tight shut, with a scream,
Ravaged by a double torture.
From the golden crown about her hair,

36

Flames shot, burning, ghastly.
But on her body so soft, the soft dress
That the children had brought began to feed.
She rose, ran, on fire, 1190
Tossing her head every way,
To shake off that halo. But it clung.
The more she shook, the more it flared.
Seared to the bone, at last she fell to the ground.
A father might recognise her, only a father.
You couldn't pick out her eyes,
Her features. Just blood dripping
From her head on to the flickering flames.
While her flesh, gorged on by the poison, 1200
Dribbled off her like gum from a pine.
Horrible. I can see it. No one dared touch her.
We were witnesses. We'd learned.
But her poor father knew nothing of this.
Rushing in he threw himself on her body,
Weeping, clinging to her, crying
'Child, poor child, who or what has destroyed you?
Who's turned this old man into a gravestone?
Oh child, let me die too.' 1210
Eventually his sobbing began to subside
And he started to try to get up.
But as he'd clung to her, she clung to him,
Like ivy clings to the laurel.
So with her dress he began a ghastly wrestling-match.
As he scrabbled to get to his knees,
She seemed to reach and grab him.
He fought her off and the flesh stripped from his bones.
At last – it took time – the wretched man
Succumbed to his fate and gave up the ghost.
The corpses lie together, child and father, close. 1220
'Let me die too.' The release of tears he craved.

And your part in this? I've said nothing.
You'll have secured your own escape.
'Walking shadows', that's all we are.
And so-called clever men, the silver-tongued –

I'm not afraid to admit it – pay too. They pay.
Call no man happy. That's what I say.
You might be luckier than your neighbour,
1230 Be more prosperous. But happy? Never.
CHORUS. Disaster on disaster heaped on Jason,
All in a single day. And he deserved it.
But for you we do feel pity, poor daughter of Creon,
Victim of Jason's wedding-plans.
MEDEA. Sisters, the die is cast. No delays.
I must kill the children and make my escape.
No delays, for them to fall into the clutches
Of some other bloody, vengeful hand.
1240 They have to die, of course. So.
I gave them life. I'll take it away again.
Steel yourself, my heart. Why wait?
Awful, but this you have to do.
Grasp the sword, vile hand. Grasp it.
The slow, short walk. To a life-sentence.
Don't weaken. Don't think of them as children,
Your children. Ignore love. For one short day
Make believe they're not your boys.
Then, then will be the time for grief.
1250 You kill them. Poor Medea. But I love them.
Exit MEDEA.
CHORUS. Come Earth, look up,
See, bright-shining Sun,
This destructive, lethal woman,
Planning infanticide.
She's family, your family,
God-blood
Under threat from men. Stop her,
Hold her back. God-born light of the Sun,
A bloody, vengeful Fury is abroad.
1260 Drive her out.

Labour a waste.
Nurturing a waste.
Medea who left behind the threatening,
Blue-black rocks,

38

What fatal passion drives her,
Irredeemable,
To contemplate this murder?
Murder in the family for mortals
Means pollution. The Earth demands
A retribution and the gods comply.   1270

FIRST CHILD (*off*). Help!
  [*Io moi.*]
CHORUS. Shouting. That's the children, surely?
  That woman, damnable woman.
FIRST CHILD (*off*). Help! Away from mother. How?
  [*Oimoi, ti drasô? Poi phugô métros cheras?*]
SECOND CHILD (*off*). Don't know. Brother! Done for.
  [*Ouk oid', adelphe philtat'; ollumestha gar.*]
CHORUS. Should I go in? Someone should save them,
  The children.
FIRST CHILD (*off*). Help us! For god's sake, help!
  [*Nai, pros theôn aréxat'; en deonti gar.*]
SECOND CHILD (*off*). Sword. Can't escape. The sword . . .
  [*Hôs engus édé g'esmen arkuôn xiphous.*]
CHORUS. She's made of stone. Of iron, damn her,
  A woman who bears children   1280
  Only, herself, to kill them.
  I've heard of one, just one,
  In the past who cut down her own children,
  Ino, driven insane
  When Hera harried her from home.
  She killed her two children, then herself.
  Poor creature, she went into the sea.
  Drowned herself from guilt.
  Can you imagine anything worse?   1290
  Sex. Passion.
  The trouble it brings.
  Enter JASON.
JASON. You, women. What are you hanging about here for?
  Is she in there? You know what she's done.
  Medea, is she there? Or has she got away?
  She'll have to tunnel her way out this time,

39

Or sprout wings and fly,
If she wants to avoid justice from the palace.
Killing the royal family!

1300   Does she think she'll get away with this?
It's the boys I'm worried about, not her.
She'll be paid back, eye for an eye,
But I mean to save my boys.
I don't want the family taking it out on them
For what that damned mother of theirs has done.

CHORUS. Oh Jason. Poor Jason. You don't know the half of it
Or you could never have spoken as you have.

JASON. Meaning? Is she going to kill me now?

CHORUS. Your sons. They're dead. Their mother killed them.

1310 JASON. What? Finished. Destroyed.

CHORUS. It's your children who are finished. Think of them.

JASON. She killed them. Where? Out here? Inside?

CHORUS. Open the doors to see the carnage.

JASON. Break in. Force your way in.
   I'll see this double horror,
Both boys dead. And the woman I mean to kill.
Enter MEDEA above.

MEDEA. Why this assault on the doors,
Looking for the bodies and their killer?
No need. Anything you want to say,

1320   Say it. You cannot touch me now.
My grandfather, the Sun, has furnished me
With a chariot to protect me from my enemies.

JASON. You plague. You hateful thing. You woman
Detested by god, by me, by every mortal man.
You dared to draw a sword and plunge it
Into children, your children, my children.
You do this and can still look at the sun
And at the earth. No crime's more monstrous.
My curse, till death. Now at last I see you as you are.

1330   I never realised when I brought you to Greece
From your home, that primitive country,
You were a traitress to your father and your land.
A degenerate. Now the gods heap retribution

On me for your slaughtering your own brother
Before you ever embarked on the good ship *Argo*.
That was only the start. We married.
You had my children. Now you've killed them.
Why? Sex, just for the sake of sex.
No Greek woman would have done it.
Yet instead of one of them I deigned to marry you.   1340
What a wife you turned out to be.
An animal, not a woman,
A savage, some prehistoric monster.
Nothing I can say would touch your sort.
Your heart's too hard.
Vile. Leave, then, drenched in your children's blood.
Leave me to grieve my fate.
No new marriage to enjoy.
Never again to speak to the boys I fathered
And brought up. A beaten man.   1350

MEDEA. We could debate at some length about this,
  I think, but there's no real point.
  Zeus knows how you've been treated and what I did.
  I deserved better than contempt for my bed,
  Rejection for something tastier. Oh, no.
  You mocked me, Jason. While that brand-new bride
  And her father Creon wanted me out of here.
  'Animal', am I? 'Not a woman.'
  'Savage. Prehistoric monster.'
  That's what it took to crush your heart.   1360

JASON. Oh, you suffer too, do you, like me?

MEDEA. Suffer, yes. You cannot mock me. That's my consolation.

JASON. What a mother, children! What an evil woman!

MEDEA. What a father, boys! Victims of that male disorder.

JASON. It wasn't my hand killed them.

MEDEA. Conceit, rather, and a second marriage.

JASON. And that's worth an execution?

MEDEA. It's just a peccadillo, is it?

JASON. To a proper wife, yes. To you everything's wrong.

MEDEA. They're dead now. I hope it hurts.   1370

JASON. They'll live on in my vengeance, never fear.

41

MEDEA. The gods recognise who started this.

JASON. They recognise a warped mind, that's for sure.

MEDEA. Detest me then. Twisted words and I reject them.

JASON. And I reject yours. I propose a truce.

MEDEA. On what terms? I'm agreeable.

JASON. Let me have the bodies to mourn and then to bury.

MEDEA. Oh no you don't. I'll bury them.
    I'll take them to Hera's precinct
1380   To save their graves from desecration.
    But I will establish a ceremony here in Corinth
    With rites to atone for this bloody deed,
    While I go to Athens
    To live under the protection of Aegeus.
    But for you, the dirty death that you deserve,
    With your skull smashed under the *Argo*.
    And the memory of that woman to your dying day.

JASON. If children are protected by a Fury,
1390   Let her and Justice consume you.

MEDEA. What power, what deity, do you think,
    Will listen to a condemned perjurer?

JASON. Child-killer!

MEDEA. Oh, go and bury your bride.

JASON. I'm going. A father, childless.

MEDEA. You don't know suffering. Wait till you're old.

JASON. Children . . .

MEDEA. My children, not yours.

JASON. Their murderer.

MEDEA. To torture you.

1400 JASON. Let me touch them. Kiss them. Just once.

MEDEA. Now you want to touch them. And kiss them, now.
    What about exile? It was a different story then.

JASON. Please. For god's sake,
    Grant me just one touch.

MEDEA. No. It's pointless to ask.

JASON. Do you hear how she rejects me?
    Do you hear, Zeus, when I've suffered
    At her savage, child-killer's hands?
    What's left for me, I'll do.

I'll mourn and call heaven to witness 1410
That you killed my children
And would not let me bury them,
Or even touch their bodies.
Would they had never been born
To die cut down by you.
Exit JASON.
CHORUS. Olympian Zeus ordains,
The gods accomplish, strangely.
Things rarely end as you expect.
The unexpected is god's way,
The lesson of this story.

THE PHOENICIAN WOMEN

Translated by David Thompson

Characters

JOCASTA, *formerly Queen of Thebes*
ANTIGONE, *her daughter*
TUTOR *to Antigone*
CHORUS *of women from Phoenicia*
POLYNEICES, *younger son of Jocasta*
ETEOCLES, *elder son of Jocasta, now King of Thebes*
CREON, *brother of Jocasta*
TEIRESIAS, *a blind prophet*
MENOECEUS, *son of Creon*
FIRST MESSENGER
SECOND MESSENGER
OEDIPUS

A shortened version of this translation was originally written for
performance by students at the Royal Academy of Dramatic Art
in the Spring term, 1967. Re-titled 'The Sons of Oedipus', it
was broadcast on BBC Radio 3, on 29 July 1976, with Siobhan
McKenna as Jocasta and Michael Redgrave as Oedipus, directed
by John Theocharis. Its first public stage performance was given
at the Greenwich Theatre, on 3 February 1977 with the
following cast:

JOCASTA	Siobhan McKenna
NARRATOR/CHORUS	Freda Dowie
ANTIGONE	Ursula Mohan
TUTOR	Patrick Hannaway
POLYNEICES	Scott Antony
ETEOCLES	Michael Deacon
CREON	Ewan Hooper
TEIRESIAS	Richard Mayes
MENOECEUS	Jonathan Warren
FIRST MESSENGER	David Brierley
SECOND MESSENGER	Frank Barrie
OEDIPUS	Denys Hawthorne

Designed by Bruno Santini
Directed by David Thompson

Scene One
Prologue.

JOCASTA. Curse on you, light of day!
  You cut your way through the stars,
  Your sun-car flashing gold, your headlong horses
  Scattering fire across our sky!
  But on that distant day
  You hung over Thebes like a doom,
  Like an omen,
  When Cadmus, from his far Phoenician shore,
  Found his way here . . .

  Cadmus it was who wed Aphrodite's daughter,
  And they had Polydorus: he in turn
  (So history tells) sired Labdacus, and he
  Was the father of Laius. Laius the King
  Was my husband. I am Menoeceus' daughter,   10
  The sister of Creon. I am Jocasta . . .

  Barren and empty – with Laius my marriage
  For years was barren, for years the house was empty.
  He went to the oracle, questioned the god,
  Begged that our union be blessed with issue.
  He had his answer –
  'Lord of Thebes and its famed horses,
  Sow not that seed. The gods have ruled against it.
  If you father a child, that child will kill you
  And all your house go down in blood.'   20
  But lust had its way, lust and wine,
  And Laius got me with child.
  He knew he had offended,
  He remembered that the god had warned him,
  And he took the babe and gave it to herdsmen
  To abandon on the high slopes of Cithaeron.

But first, to tether it, he spiked its ankles
With an iron skewer. That's how it got its name.
The child was later known as 'swollen foot',
And that in Greece is – OEDIPUS.

But horse–tenders from across the border,
Ranging the hills, discovered it,
And took it home, and gave it to their queen.
30   She suckled the babe I laboured for, persuaded
Her husband it was hers. And so my son grew up.
Perhaps he guessed something. Perhaps he heard the story.
But with the first flush of his young beard upon him
He was fretting to know more – who were his parents?
He set out for the oracle of Phoebus,
And so, for the second time, did Laius,
My husband Laius, needing to be reassured
The child he had exposed no longer lived.
They met, the two of them,
Met at the crossroads on the way to Phocis.
Laius' driver ordered the stranger out of his way,
40   'Stand aside for the King there!' –
But Oedipus came on. Never answered.
Not to be demeaned.
And the horses jibbed, reared,
Hooves hit his heel, that heel, drew blood . . .
Oh, what does the telling matter?
There is only the outcome, the catastrophe.
Son slew his father –
And he took the chariot home and
Gave it to him who was, he thought, his father . . .

It was after that the Sphinx came, terrorising Thebes,
Plundering her people, when they no longer
Had a king, their queen no husband.
So Creon my brother had heralds give it out
That he who could read the Sphinx's riddle should have me.
50   And who was it mastered that she-devil's rhyme
But my son Oedipus,

And was rewarded with all honour and power
And crowned King of Thebes,
And married her who bore him,
Never knowing, poor wretch,
As she never knew herself, a mother
Coupling with her child . . .
So to my son I bore sons,
Eteocles and my fine, my famous Polyneices.
And two girls – Ismene whom her father named,
And the elder named Antigone by me.
But when he learned the truth,
Knew his marriage-bed was where he had been born,
Knew he was the root and heart of all disaster,   60
He tried to tear the horror from himself,
Searching in the sockets of his eyes with needles
Till they burst blood . . .

They locked him away, my sons, when they were grown,
Shuffled him out of sight to try and forget,
Try and quiet the questions that troubled conscience.
But Oedipus lives on, in the house here,
His grief grown cancerous within him,
And always he curses his sons
So that they shrink with the terror of it –
'Inherit my house? No, inherit from me
The sword and the sword's edge. Share that between you!'
Even a blasphemy is heard in heaven.
If they stayed together, the gods might heed it.   70
So they made a pact, that first Polyneices,
Being the younger, agree to leave Thebes
While his brother remain and rule – each year to change.
But once secure, once in power, Eteocles
Would not be thrust from his throne.
Polyneices was banished. He went to Argos
And won himself there a royal bride.
Now, with the might of Argos mustered behind him,
He has come again, marching against us,
Claiming his father's throne and what is owed him.   80

I shall try to undo their quarrel. I have persuaded
Son to meet son under letters of truce
Before battle flares. And he'll come.
My messenger brings me word that he'll come.
O Zeus, hidden from us in the brightness of heaven,
You who are all-powerful, all-wise, you cannot
Forever deny all blessing to one poor mortal.
Save us, O Zeus! Hear my prayer.
Grant that my sons be reconciled . . .

Scene Two
The Watchers on the Roof

TUTOR. Highness, are you there? Fair flower of Oedipus' house
    That you are, your mother has given permission, Antigone –
90   She has said you may leave your maiden chamber
    To go up on the roof, to the very top,
    So you can see the Argive army
    Just as you asked. But wait now, wait! First
    I must reconnoitre. I want no townsfolk
    Meeting us out in the street and gossiping.
    What they say doesn't matter to me, I'm a servant,
    But you – are a princess. Oh, I've so much to tell you
    About meeting your brother, taking
    The Queen your mother's offer of truce to him,
    The things I saw in the Argive camp, and heard . . .
100   Good, there's no one about. We'll try the old stairs
    Of cedar wood. Watch where you're putting your feet.
    The view from up here takes in the whole plain
    And along by the river as far as the spring of Dirce.
    You'll get an idea how vast their army is.
ANTIGONE. Please give me your hand, I need your hand . . .
TUTOR. Youth calls on age, does it?
ANTIGONE. It's steep up the last step . . .
TUTOR. Here, take hold, lass – up you come!
    Just in time too. It's starting to move.
    The army's on the move. It's splitting up
    Into battalions . . .

ANTIGONE. O Artemis, protect us! The whole wide plain   110
  Is flashing bronze!
TUTOR. Oh, yes. Your brother
  Didn't mean us to be unimpressed,
  Bringing such ranks of horse and infantry
  Against us.
ANTIGONE. Can our gates hold them? Are the brazen bolts
  Secure? The old stone walls?
TUTOR. Never fear. Inside the city all's safe.
  Now mark that first man, remember him well.
ANTIGONE. The one with the white crest out in front?   120
  So, who is he? He carries that great bronze shield
  As if it weighed nothing.
TUTOR. A famous captain, my lady.
ANTIGONE. Where from? What's his name?
TUTOR. He comes from Mycenae. A proud family.
  They have lands along the river Lerna.
  He's the Lord Hippomedon.
ANTIGONE. Oh, he looks arrogant.
  He frightens me, like those giants in pictures
  Who stand on mountaintops and throw thunderbolts.
  As though he weren't human.   130
TUTOR. Do you see the one crossing the river?
ANTIGONE. The foreign one with that strange armour?
  Who is he?
TUTOR. Tydeus.
ANTIGONE. Tydeus? Who became brother to my brother,
  To my Polyneices, when they married sisters?
  He looks so – different. He's armed like some
  Wild tribesman.
TUTOR. He's from Aetolia, child.
  They all carry target-shields like that,
  And those throwing-spears. They're deadly marksmen.   140
ANTIGONE. You know so much about them. Where
  Did you learn it all?
TUTOR. In their camp,
  When I met your brother. I learned their ensigns.
ANTIGONE. But who's that skirting the Zetheus monument,

With the flowing hair and fierce eyes? He's so young
To command them. But look how the soldiers
Press at his heels and throng about him.
150 TUTOR. That's Parthenopaeus, Atalanta's son.
ANTIGONE. May Artemis, who hunts the hills with his mother,
Shoot him down like a wild beast for coming
To lay waste my city!
TUTOR. I pray so too, child.
Yet the cause that brings them is not unjust,
And the gods may see that. That's my fear.
ANTIGONE. Where's he
Who was born to such pain, to so many troubles,
Who shares one mother with me? Dear tutor,
Dear, dear tutor, point me out Polyneices.
TUTOR. Over there, near the tomb to Niobe's daughters.
160 He stands at Adrastus' side. Can you see him?
ANTIGONE. Yes, I see. Not clearly, but I can see
A remembered shape, the hint of him.
Oh, could I fly to him, race down the wind to him,
To my own dear brother, and fling my arms
Round his neck, and kiss away all that time
Of exile and suffering. Isn't he glorious
In his golden war-gear? He dazzles like the sun
In the morning!
170 TUTOR. He'll be here soon. The truce
Will bring him. Your heart won't be empty long.
ANTIGONE. And who is that one, driving the chariot
With white horses?
TUTOR. That is the priest-king, Amphiaraos,
Bringing the animals for sacrifice, with which
To appease this land.
ANTIGONE. He reminds me somehow
Of the full moon, sailing high, shedding
Her mellow light. He rides on so serenely.
But where's the one who's always shouting
180 Terrible threats and taunting us? Where's Capaneus?
TUTOR. Down there, below, at the foot of the bastion,
Busy gauging how high the walls are, and if

They're built so he could scale them.
ANTIGONE. O Nemesis, you know the way to smother,
  A man's boasting. One bolt from Zeus,
  One lightning-flash of his wrath, and that mouth
  Would be stopped for ever. Didn't he promise
  His prize would be the daughters of Thebes
  To take home and give to the wives of Mycenae –
  That he'd net us like birds and give us away
  As bondslaves? Never, oh never, never, great   190
  Goddess of us who bear children, I beg you,
  Golden-haired daughter of Zeus, subject us to slavery!
TUTOR. Come, child, come now, it's time to go in.
  Let us go down again, back to your room
  Where it's quiet and safe. You've got what you asked for,
  Seen what you came to see. Crowds are gathering.
  The town is troubled, and womenfolk press
  Round the palace. Save me from censuring tongues
  If one of them sees you! They'll turn it into a scandal.   200
  Oh, why must women so love speaking ill of each other?

CHORAL ODE 1
  Far away left far behind now
  the city I set sail from.
  I bade farewell to Tyre and the sea-swell
  greeted me,
  carried me from my Phoenician shore.
  Apollo called me, they were sending me
  to serve him –
  was I not chosen, favoured, singled out
  Phoenicia's gift to him
  to serve him at his Delphic shrine
  below the snow-topped peaks of Parnassus?
  And swift oars sped me
  up the Ionian Sea past
  the unharvestable deeps off Sicily,   210
  while wild winds roared out of the west
  with heavenly clamour
  like chariots racing . . .

55

And I came to Cadmus' land –
I who was chosen for Apollo
beauty's prize of all my city,
came here to Thebes which Cadmus founded
Cadmus the son of Agenor . . .
I who am also of the race of Agenor
here to the towered town of his famous sons.
But I should be now in Apollo's service
adorning his temple
220   clad all in gold like the statues there –
Delphi still waits for me
to dip my hair in its sacred spring
in dedication . . .

O sacred Rock I long for you, flaming
with fire double-tongued above Delphi,
the dance of Dionysus on the heights!
And you yielding – o miracle of the vine –
230   your one ripe swelling cluster
day by day renewed
for Dionysus!
Holiest of holies I long for you,
cave of the dragon!
You mountain watch-towers of the gods themselves,
and you, Parnassus-peak snowmantled,
god-haunted!
Would that I too were treading
that deathless dance,
would that I too
were where Apollo dwells
at the hollow mid-point of the world,
and I were far from here,
and this dread taken from me . . .

For now there's War himself
240   marching against us – look!
parading before the walls.
Can you feel it, the lust for battle

rising . . .?
This is a time of blood and fire.
Oh save this city!
We cling together
one love one fear
one nation in mourning.
If this dear land of tall towers
should suffer –
one blood one race
descended all
from the horn'd moon-maiden Io,
we share one agony . . .

Thick now as thunderclouds   250
the war-shields surge and settle round the town.
It's the signal for red battle.
You wait for that don't you, War God?
It's you brings the Furies' curse
on the sons of Oedipus . . .
Oh I dread the power of Argos
and what heaven will do.
There's a man on his way here now,
armed – look! a man finding his way home,   260
and the gods know what his quarrel is
and they know it is not unjust . . .

Scene Three
The Meeting of Two Brothers

POLYNEICES. The warders slipped the bolts and let me through.
    No trouble. So, inside the walls. Now
    Is the time to fear. They have me in their net
    And I may not get out again unbloodied.
    Be wary. Watch for the trap. This side, that side.
    Sword drawn and eager. Let no man tempt it!
    Who's there?
    Or was it a noise scared me? Set foot   270
    Once on enemy soil and each thing

57

Threatens you, whatever you dare.
My mother persuaded me to this,
This coming here under truce. Well, I trust her.
Or do I trust her? Ah, here's sanctuary . . .
An altar. And women in front of the palace.
So. Back in its blind scabbard goes my sword.
I'll ask who they are. Strangers – I see you *are* strangers –
Where are you from? What do you do in Greece?

280 CHORUS. We are Phoenicians, sir – sent to serve
At Apollo's shrine, but caught here on our way
When Argos marched against Thebes. And you –
Who may you be, venturing here?

POLYNEICES. I am known to the people of Thebes. My father,
Oedipus the son of Laius: my mother,

290 The Queen Jocasta. I am Polyneices.

CHORUS. O my lord, you have come,
You who are kin to the sons of Agenor
Who sent me . . .
Master, let me fall on my knees before you,
Let me give thanks and honour you
After the custom of my people.
At last you have come to your own land again!
Queen Jocasta, come out, come out!
Open the gates!
Mother of him who has come again,
Can you not hear us?
Oh, why do you tarry within there
And not come out

300 And wind your son in your arms!

JOCASTA. I hear you. I can hear your foreign babbling.
I come. Old, slow and unsteady, but I come.
O my son . . .
At last. After such uncountable days
To look on you. Embrace your mother.
Hold me close, close . . .
Oh, the touch of you . . .
Lean down, let me feel your face,
Let me feel the dark curls nestle at my neck,

Overshadow me . . .
Oh, my darling, past hope, past dreaming of . . .   310
My son in my arms . . .
What words are there? How shall I grasp it all,
Hold on to such happiness,
Each shift and shade of it, so precious . . .
How can hand, tongue . . .
It dances with me so, to and fro . . .
I had almost forgotten . . .
You left your home so empty.
Yes, I know, you were driven away,
Your brother abused you,
But those you loved longed for you,   320
Thebes itself longed for you.
I cut my hair and wept,
Gave myself up to grief –
The white I once wore, child,
Is not for me now.
I dress in rags now,
Rags and black night.
And the old, blind man in the house here,
Since the pair of you broke away,
Has only his pain and one longing he clings to,   330
How he can kill himself,
Swift sword or a rope in the dark roof,
And curses himself for cursing his sons,
And cries out, and weeps,
And hides in his darkness.
But you, son – is it true what they tell me?
That you're married? That you've pledged yourself,
Pledged the name of your children, to foreigners   340
And foreign ways? Oh no, that was wrong.
It wrongs me, your mother, and it wrongs
The memory of Laius, a marriage like that
Far, far from home. What good can that come to?
A happy mother should raise the marriage-torch
At her son's wedding. But I was not there.
The waters of Ismenus never ran for your anointing,

There was no singing in Thebes to bring your bride home . . .
350   It's all wrong, wrong. O God, put an end to it!
This fighting, this jealousy and hate,
Your father's guilt – is that the cause?
This madness that riots through our house
Like drunken devils –
I suffer for all of it, all the pain of it
Gathers upon me.

CHORUS. From the terror of birth to the terror of losing,
A mother's care
Clings to her child. So, always.

POLYNEICES. Mother, what brought me here?
Why have I come, in my right mind and yet
Without thinking, here where my enemies are?
It's because we can't help ourselves. There's a
Yearning for home compels every one of us –
And those who say anything else do not know,
360   They're toying with words. I was frightened to come,
Frightened of treachery and of my brother,
Frightened of death. I came through my city
With drawn sword and eyes all around me.
One thing kept me going – my trust in you
And the truce you made to draw me inside these walls.
But I came full of tears, after all this time
Seeing the houses again, the altars,
The schoolrooms where I spent my boyhood,
The river Dirce – all I have been cheated of
And driven away from, to live in a city
370   Which would never be mine, and waste my years weeping.
And yet what is past grief to this grief – to see you
With shaved head and black dress of mourning?
O God, have pity on me!
How terrible is hatred, mother, between those
Who belong together. How hard the healing of it.
What does my father do now, here in his palace,
He who sees darkness? What of my sisters?
Do they feel for me in my exile's misery?

JOCASTA. There's surely a god destroying us, one by one.

And I was the start of it. I bore what was   380
Forbidden. Married your father and had you.
But what of that now? The gods dispose
And we must bear it. Yet I yearn to know –
But I fear to ask, I fear its hurt . . .
POLYNEICES. Ask what you will, mother. Do not
　Leave it unsaid. Your wish is my wish.
JOCASTA. It haunts me what exile has been to you.
POLYNEICES. Hard to bear. Hardest of all things.
　A cruel word and a crueller fate.
JOCASTA. In what most cruel?   390
POLYNEICES. You are never a free man. The tongue is fettered.
JOCASTA. A man can utter his thought. He's not a slave.
POLYNEICES. Ah, but we serve masters. We're subject
　To their whim, dependent on them.
JOCASTA. If they're fools, you must suffer them?
POLYNEICES. Exiles are beggars, and to gain their ends,
　Despite themselves, must ape the slave's style.
JOCASTA. They say that exiles always have hope to feed on.
POLYNEICES. Hope has bright eyes to see the future, yes.
　It keeps you waiting, though. Waiting for ever!
JOCASTA. Then does not time prove that hope is empty?
POLYNEICES. Perhaps. And yet when everything is black
　It has a kind of beauty.
JOCASTA. Later you married. That kept you fed.   400
　What fed you before that?
POLYNEICES. Sometimes I ate, sometimes I fasted.
　I lived from day to day.
JOCASTA. But your father had friends – didn't they help you?
POLYNEICES. Look for friends when you prosper. You have
　　　　　　　　　　　　　　　　none when you don't.
JOCASTA. You're of royal blood. Did that give you no standing?
POLYNEICES. How could it do so? I am dispossessed.
　My birth never won me a crust of bread!
JOCASTA. It does seem true there's nowhere men can trust
　But their own dear land, their home.
POLYNEICES. Words can't express how much it means.
JOCASTA. But you went to Argos. How, my son? Why?

POLYNEICES. Why? I don't know. Some god, was it,
  Called me there? Fate?
JOCASTA. In all things there's some divine purpose. You found
                                        there
  A bride. How was that?
POLYNEICES. Adrastus heard an oracle.
410 JOCASTA. 'Heard an oracle'? What do you mean?
POLYNEICES. 'Marry your daughters,' it said, 'to the boar and
                                     the lion.'
JOCASTA. What have wild brutes' names to do with you?
POLYNEICES. It was night when I knocked at Adrastus' gate . . .
JOCASTA. Looking for a bed, poor wandering one?
POLYNEICES. Yes. But then there arrived a second refugee.
JOCASTA. In as awful plight as you were? Who was he?
POLYNEICES. Tydeus, son of Oeneus.
420 JOCASTA. But why did you seem to Adrastus like wild beasts?
POLYNEICES. We'd fought over a mattress. Like two beasts.
JOCASTA. He was reminded of the oracle . . .?
POLYNEICES. And gave us two his two young daughters.
JOCASTA. Have they brought you happiness, these marriages?
POLYNEICES. We have blameless wives. They still content us.
JOCASTA. Now you have rallied an army to your cause.
  What made them follow you here?
POLYNEICES. The King Adrastus has sworn to restore
  Both his two sons-in-law, Tydeus and me,
  Each to his own home. I am the first.
  They are all here to help me –
430 From Mycenae, from Argos, mighty men all –
  Help which I hate but I need.
  This is Thebes, my Thebes, I march against . . .
  Do you hear me, gods? It was never my will
  That spear of mine should be levelled
  Against those that raised me, those I love.
  Mother, we look to you. You are the only one
  To unravel this web of disaster,
  To knit us in love again, as we were born,
  And rescue us all – me, you, this city.
440 Haven't they always said, what belongs to a man

Is what wins him honour? And possession is power?
I say so too. That's why I am here,
To reclaim my own. What use is birth to a beggar?
CHORUS. Look, look, the meeting is made up. Here now
   Comes Eteocles. Jocasta, it rests with you.
   You are the mother of these two.
   Have you the words to reconcile them?
ETEOCLES. Yes, mother? You called. I am here. I come for your
                                     sake.
   What do we have to do? Will someone begin?
   Come, the city's defences wait on me.
   I have interrupted my preparations
   To hear what you had to say. Wasn't that why   450
   You prevailed on me to let this creature
   Enter our walls?
JOCASTA. Stop, Eteocles, stop it. You cannot be hasty
   And be just. Slow words for wisdom's sake.
   Check that impatience in your heart, that anger
   In your eye. What do you think you see?
   Medusa's head? This is your brother.
   Your brother come again. You too, Polyneices.
   Turn and face him. How can you speak to him
   Or listen to him if you will not look at him?
   I wish to advise you wisely, both of you.   460
   When friends who have quarrelled come together,
   Meet face to face, they have to think
   Of one thing only – what they came for.
   Nothing else. The past and past wrongs
   Must have no place in their remembrance.
   Son Polyneices, you shall speak first.
   You have come here at the head of an Argive army
   Claiming you suffer injustice. Now God
   Be our judge and settle this strife for us.
POLYNEICES. Truth is so simple. A just cause
   Needs no devious defence. It argues   470
   Its own rightness. It is the wrong
   Which is so sickly weak it can't stand up
   Without the help of dubious doctoring.

I cared for the future of my father's house.
It was in both our interests – mine and my brother's.
I wanted to escape the fate that Oedipus
Had cursed us with, and voluntarily
I left this land and I surrendered
To this man here the kingship of it
For a year's cycle, so that in turn
I might myself resume it, and not
Involve us both in hatred and violence,
480 Doing and suffering harm.
But that is what happened.
He agreed with the idea, he swore an oath
Before the gods, but then did nothing he promised.
He will not resign the throne and usurps
My share of my own house.
Now I am prepared, given what is mine,
To withdraw and disband my army,
Reoccupy my home for the allotted span,
Yielding it once again for an equal period
To him, and not to bring my scaling-ladders
Against the proud towers of Thebes,
Nor raze them and this city to the ground
490 As I *will* do if justice is denied me –
As I will surely do. The gods are my witness
That, having in all things acted justly,
I most unjustly have my homeland stolen from me.
It is an offense against heaven.
That is my grievance, mother. You have heard it
As it is, without elaboration.
I hardly think the dullest mind
Could fail to recognise the justice of it.
CHORUS. I listen as one not born a Greek,
But feel his cause is soundly reasoned.
500 ETEOCLES. If we all thought alike, there'd be no argument.
Justice? Rights? Men do not know such things.
They give them names, they do not act by them.
Let me be frank, mother. I will hide nothing.
I want one thing,

64

And I would pluck the sun and stars out of the sky
Or rake the underworld, to see I had it.
That thing is power, the power to be a king –
Something too precious, mother, to barter
With a brother when it is mine, I hold it.
What sort of weakness would it be
To let the great thing slip and settle
For a smaller? And to *him*, who comes here   510
Threatening violence and trampling with armies
Over our country? I could not stoop to it.
It would be shaming Thebes itself to hand him
My throne because I winced
At the sight of Argive spears. The wrong
Is his, mother, trying to negotiate
By force. Words will win all the sword can.
If on some other terms he wishes to live here
He may. But I will not consent,
When I might be king, to be his subject.   520
Let him do his worst. Let fire and sword
Take their course. Harness the horses. Fill
The plain with chariots. He knows I will not yield.
And if this is wrong, then wrong is best done
For a throne. Save morality for issues less tremendous.
JOCASTA. O son, O Eteocles – I am old, I know it . . .
Don't despise me for that, not now, not altogether . . .
We who have experience can sometimes
Speak wiser than youth. Oh why, child,   530
Grasp so at greatness? Do not. Ambition
Is the very soul of wrong. It enters in
Where there is harmony and happiness
And tears them apart, this spirit that drives *you*.
Others have rights too. Respect them. It were better
Far to do so. How is friend ever bound
To friend, city to city or ally to ally
Except as equals? How but as equals
Can men share this world as nature intended?
To have or have not, to be greater or less –
Each is foe to the other. Set them up

65

540   And the days of hate dawn.
Do we not weigh, measure, number our lives
By due proportion, by allotted share?
Does not night's dark eye divide with day
An equal pacing of their yearly round
Without resentment that each gives place to other?
They serve their turn humbly, night and day – but you!
You cannot bear to halve your inheritance
With him who inherited with you. Where's justice then?
You value kingship too much, though what is kingship
But power enjoyed above justice? Oh, why

550   Do you think it so great? Do you wish that men
Look up to you? Vainglorious wish!
Is it wealth you desire with all its cares?
What's wealth? 'More', only that. Just a word.
If you understood better, you'd know that enough
Is sufficient. We do not own our possessions
On this earth. We simply hold in trust
What the gods have given. And when they want,
They'll require them of us again. Wealth
Is not lasting. It's only for a day.
Come, if I put before you a choice,

560   And ask if you would be king or saviour of your city,
Would you say 'king'? But if this man beats you
And Thebes goes under when Argos attacks,
You will see this city smashed apart,
You will see its women raped by Argive soldiers
And dragged off for slaves
And Thebes will have only curses left
For that power you pursue, and all your greatness.
And you, Polyneices –
What misthought favours has Adrastus done you?

570   You were mad to come here. Would you sack Thebes?
Think . . .
If you win, which God forbid, how before heaven
Will you fashion your thank-offering to Zeus?
With what words will you dedicate the sacrifice
Of your conquered country? How will your trophies

66

Be inscribed – 'Polyneices has burned Thebes
And to the gods offers these shields' – thus?
O my son, don't give that memory to Greece!
And yet if you fail, if his cause overruns you,
How will you go again to Argos, leaving here
Thousands of Argive dead? Will they not say
'Fatal the wedding you gave your daughter, Adrastus.   580
For one girl's marriage, see – we are destroyed!'
O child, both courses you pursue are fatal –
You lose Argos or lose Thebes. Let go, let go,
The two of you. Don't reach too far. Two madnesses
Colliding crushes us all . . .

CHORUS. O all you powers above, prevent such terrors,
And set these sons of Oedipus at one!

ETEOCLES. No, mother, words are no use any longer.
We've wasted our time
And your goodwill gains us nothing.
I've laid down the only terms we could agree on –   590
I remain king here. I rule in Thebes.
So leave off your wearisome admonitions,
Let me be.
As for you – I warn you
To get out before you are killed.

POLYNEICES. Before I am killed? Who would kill me?
Who bears such a charmed life that
He could draw sword on me
Before getting killed himself?

ETEOCLES. I do.

POLYNEICES. I thought you would think so. But creatures like
                                                                    you
Who cling to power, cling to life.

ETEOCLES. You come mightily supported against one
You rate so lowly.

POLYNEICES. The better general is he who's best prepared.

ETEOCLES. You take advantage of the truce to be arrogant.   600
It is all that saves you from death.

POLYNEICES. It saves you too. This one last time,
I claim from you my right and my throne.

ETEOCLES. I know of no claim. I stand by what is mine.

POLYNEICES. By what is more than yours . . .

ETEOCLES. I have spoken. The city waits for you to leave.

POLYNEICES. O altars of my fathers . . .

ETEOCLES. Which you're prepared to plunder . . .

POLYNEICES. Hear me!

ETEOCLES. Why should they hear you when you march against
them?

POLYNEICES. O temples of the gods of shining steeds . . .

ETEOCLES. Who loathe your name!

POLYNEICES. He denies me the land of my birth . . .

ETEOCLES. You came to destroy it.

POLYNEICES. It is unjust, O heaven, unjust!

ETEOCLES. Call on Mycenae's gods, not ours.

POLYNEICES. You were born godless.

ETEOCLES. But not, I think, my country's enemy.

POLYNEICES. No? When you cheat me and drive me out of it?

610 ETEOCLES. And intend to kill you. You forgot that.

POLYNEICES. Oedipus, my father, do you hear the wrongs I
suffer?

ETEOCLES. He hears the wrongs you *do*.

POLYNEICES. And you, my mother . . .

ETEOCLES. Her name should scald your tongue.

POLYNEICES. O my city . . .

ETEOCLES. Go. Go to Argos. Call on her.

POLYNEICES. I am going. Never fear. Mother, I thank you . . .

ETEOCLES. Get out of this city!

POLYNEICES. Let me see my father.

ETEOCLES. Never.

POLYNEICES. My sisters . . .

ETEOCLES. You'll not set eyes on them again.

POLYNEICES. O my sisters . . .

ETEOCLES. You call on them? You're their worst enemy.

POLYNEICES. Mother, farewell.

JOCASTA. Son, I can only fare in sorrow.

POLYNEICES. I am son of yours no longer . . .

JOCASTA. Is there no end . . .?

620 POLYNEICES. For this man dishonours me.

68

ETEOCLES. You are my dishonour.
POLYNEICES. Where will your battle-station be?
ETEOCLES. Why?
POLYNEICES. I will take my stand against you there, to kill you.
ETEOCLES. Good! We are of one mind at last!
JOCASTA. Oh no, my children, what will you do?
POLYNEICES. You will see.
JOCASTA. The curse of Oedipus!
ETEOCLES. Ruin seize all our house!
POLYNEICES. The time comes, it comes soon, when my sword
  Will be urgent with death. But the land that nursed me
                                  knows,
  The gods above know, how piteously I have suffered.
  They see, yes, they see me now shamefully used,
  Not like a son of Oedipus, like a slave, spurned,
  Thrust out, dishonoured. Thebes, whatever becomes of you,
  You know I am not to blame – it is this man!
  This is the guilty man! I came here unwilling   630
  And unwilling leave. Apollo of the Crossways, I leave you.
  I leave you, city I love, friends of my youth, statues
  Of the gods we fed with offerings. Perhaps I will never
  See you again. But my heart's hope is awake and eager –
  This man must be killed, and I shall rule in Thebes!
ETEOCLES. Out! Get out! How truly our father called you
                               'Polyneices' –
  The 'man of strife'. The gods must have warned him of you!

CHORAL ODE II.
  Once there was no city here
  till Cadmus came
  Cadmus of Tyre came searching
  from far Phoenicia searching.
  There will be a sign given the god had said –
  a heifer a wandering heifer   640
  unbroken knowing no master.
  Follow, and where it stops
  that is your place,
  where it kneels and salutes the earth

build there your house.
The plain is harvest-heavy there
sweet streams gush from a grateful soil
the waters of Dirce tumble through meadows
green with springing seed –
it is where the great god Bacchus was born
650   when Zeus's lightning flashed through his mother's side,
where with slow-twining tendrils
the ivy wove a bower of green shadow
over the growing child
for the maidens of Thebes to worship ever after
in song
when they call in the Bacchic dance his name
Evoe!

And so it happened,
and Cadmus came down to the stream called Dirce
for consecration.
And there was a dragon there to guard it
the War God's dragon
threatening death in the glittering eye
660   that scanned and scanned the forbidden waters . . .
A blow a great rock the head
crushed smashed –
with a hero's strength he killed it
Cadmus killed it . . .
Then there came in his mind's ear the voice
of the goddess Pallas Athene prompting –
'Pull the dragon's teeth from its jaw
and like seed
scatter them over the furrowed earth . . .'
670   He took them scattered them and there rose
out of the black earth a terror, it sent up a harvest
of spear-tips crests shields swords
a race of warriors full-armed growing out of the ground
sprouting over the fruitful plain
in anger.
And slaughter raced among them

70

raced blind among them iron-hearted
giving them back to the earth that bore them
drenching with their blood the soil that briefly
briefly had sent them into the sun and showed them
once to the winds of heaven . . .
Till half remained, till half remaining
laid their swords at the feet of Cadmus
and bound themselves to him to build this city.

Epaphos, hear us!
child of Io child of Zeus
hear us crying with foreign tongues!   680
Come down come down
to the land you loved,
the race that raised to you this city,
who are your sons.
And you Mother Earth, Demeter, Persephone
ruler of all, nurse of all
that springs from the soil
send the flame of your sacred torch
blazing through this land
and protect it and defend it,
o gods who can do
all things!

Scene Four
The Preparations for Battle

ETEOCLES. Bring Creon here, the Queen my mother's brother.   690
  Tell him I wish his counsel on matters
  Touching the state and on ourselves
  Before the raised spear calls us into battle –
  But no, he saves you the journey. I see him coming . . .
CREON. Sir, I have been everywhere, round all
  The city gates and every sentry, trying to find you.
ETEOCLES. And I, Creon, needed to see you. I met my brother   700
  And heard his terms of peace. They are quite worthless.
CREON. I was told so. Thebes is now, it seems, too small

71

For his ambition, with Adrastus behind him
And such an army. But that's as God wills.
My information is more pressing.

ETEOCLES. And what may that be?

CREON. We have an Argive prisoner . . .

ETEOCLES. Who can tell us what they're up to?

710 CREON. They're planning to encircle us, to throw
A ring of steel round the whole city.

ETEOCLES. Then we must attack. Now. Waste no time about it.

CREON. You are impetuous, sir. Where would we attack,
How would we attack?

ETEOCLES. Across the moat. We can get at them there.

CREON. But our forces are weak. Theirs are strong.

ETEOCLES. Come, Creon, I know them. Their courage is
Where their mouths are.

CREON. Sire, Argos is famed and feared throughout all Greece.

ETEOCLES. You are too timid. I'd fill the plain up with their
dead.

CREON. I hope so. Indeed. But such a task
Would not be . . . unlaborious.

720 ETEOCLES. I'll not keep my army cooped up in this city
Doing nothing.

CREON. But we do need to plan, to deliberate wisely.
It is our only hope of victory.

ETEOCLES. You want me to consider other ways?

CREON. All other ways. We dare not depend on one alone.

ETEOCLES. What about an ambush, attacking by night?

CREON. As long as our retreat's secured, if it should fail.

ETEOCLES. You can't count on certainty at night, but
Attack does give you the advantage.

CREON. And it's more terrible at night if things go wrong.

ETEOCLES. All right, then. Take them around supper-time
And rush them with infantry.

CREON. A surprise, a brief skirmish. We need to annihilate
them.

730 ETEOCLES. They couldn't retreat. The river Dirce's too deep.

CREON. None of this helps to safeguard ourselves.

ETEOCLES. What about a cavalry charge against the main camp?

72

CREON. It's impregnable. It has a ring of chariots round it.
ETEOCLES. Dear gods! What am I supposed to do then?
  Just hand the city to them?
CREON. No . . . no, of course not. But no prudent policy
  Was ever built on a string of extravagant ideas.
ETEOCLES. Suggest a more prudent policy than my 'ideas'.
CREON. They say – I have been told – that seven of their
                                           number . . .
ETEOCLES. Seven? What can they do with seven?
CREON. . . . That seven have been chosen to lead a force
  Against each of our seven gates.
ETEOCLES. And what do we do? Wait for them, helplessly?   740
CREON. You choose seven also, one for each gate.
ETEOCLES. With men at their command? Or are they
  To be champions, and fight solo?
CREON. With men at their command. Select the best.
ETEOCLES. They'll need the best. They'll have scaling attempts
  Against the walls to deal with.
CREON. Also captains under them, so they can delegate
                                           responsibility.
ETEOCLES. And am I to appoint them for their courage
  Or because they're good at 'policy' and plans?
CREON. Both, sir. Neither can survive without the other.
ETEOCLES. All right, we'll do it. I'll go round our seven gates
  As you suggest, and set a chosen man at each
  With forces to match what the enemy sets against him.   750
  I'll name them later – now would be wasting time
  With Argives camping beneath our very walls.
  But the one they set against me, God willing,
  Will be my brother. I am the one must fight him,
  Subdue him to my spear. I must kill the traitor
  Who comes here expecting to sack my city.
  Creon, before I go – should anything happen to me,
  I ratify herewith the marriage of my sister   760
  Antigone to your son Haemon. See to it.
  And you are my mother's brother. Need I say –
  Look after her, for your sake and for mine.
  My father I can't commend. His blinding

73

He brought on himself and he must live with it,
While we . . . his curse could kill us yet.
That's one thing we've not done. Summon Teiresias.
He could tell us about that, he might have a prophecy
Or an oracle or something about it . . .
770   I'll send your boy Menoeceus to fetch him.
He'll come sweetly for you, Creon, he'll talk to you.
But I've mocked his magic and mumbo-jumbo
Too often to his face. He bears me a grudge.
One charge I lay on you, Creon – on you
And this city. If our side wins, the body
Of Polyneices is not to be buried in Thebes,
Ever. Make the penalty death if it's tried,
And whoever tries it, however trusted.
I leave this with you. Now call out my guards.
780   Bring out my arms and armour. We go into battle.
The fight before us is a fight for justice
And victory will be ours. Let us pray
For the safety of the city. O spirit of wisdom,
Of all grace, kindest of gods, fair counsellor,
Protect us and take us now into thy care.

CHORAL ODE III.
War – war and death
panic and blood and death . . .
Tie up your hair put away the flute
stifle the song in your throat
stop the dancing
all the sweet service of Dionysus.
War calls another tune and a different dance
without flutes.
There are Argive armies snuffing the air
790   for our blood,
there's a rattle of harness a clatter of hooves
and chariots thundering up past the bend in the river,
men are massing beneath the old stone walls
and they dance with shields, they sing to the sword
and they hate us.

Thebes has known nothing but trouble.   800
Up there among the secret glens on Cithaeron
up near the snow-line peer through the leaves
scatter the shy things in their thickets
and what will you find?
A child cradled a babe
with the scars of gold hooks on him –
Oedipus.
Who was never meant to live.
Why did he have to live?
Then another affliction –
the witch-bird swooping down from the high crags
the Sphinx screeching out of the sky
clinging with clawed hands and clawed feet
to the ramparts
snatching away our children
off into the untrodden blue.
Hell sent her against Thebes.   810
Why was she sent?

And now new strife new discord
because two brothers quarrel,
rampant like a poisonous weed
in the house of Oedipus
all through the city
from the fault of a birth a blinding
an incestuous bed . . .

Can you win through, city of the Dragon Men –
can you pluck honour out of your shame   820
find a new glory in your ancient grief?
You once knew a day when the Sons of Heaven
stood all around at Cadmus' wedding feast,
you knew a day when Dirce and Ismenus
watering the green plain at your feet
heard Amphion's lyre raise your walls to music.
Yes, Thebes had kings descended from Io
as I am descended.

75

830   Once Thebes stood high
      and was honoured and was glorious
      and war crowned her with triumph.

Scene Five
The Prophecy of Teiresias

TEIRESIAS. On, daughter, lead on. You are the eye
    For my blind steps like a star is to sailors.
    Forward. But keep to the level places
    So I don't stumble. I don't feel very strong.
    You have my writing-tablets? And the lots
840   I was casting at my seat of prophecy
    To chart the oracles the birds were giving me?
    Hold them safe. Where's Creon's son?
    I hope it's not much further to the city
    And your honoured parent, young Menoeceus?
    My knees are folding under me. I've come so far
    I can't go on much longer.
CREON. Hold up, Teiresias,
    You've come to port now. You're among your friends.
    Take his arm, Menoeceus. Old men and mule-carts –
    Both alike! Won't move if there's no hand to help them.
TEIRESIAS. Creon? Oh, so we're here. Why the urgent
                             summons?
850 CREON. All in good time. I'm not forgetting it.
    Get your breath back first. Throw off
    The way's weariness and collect yourself.
TEIRESIAS. I'm worn out with work. Yes. Only yesterday
    I was away helping Erechtheus' sons.
    They had a war on too. Against Eumolpus.
    I gave victory to them. See this gold crown I'm wearing?
    They gave it to me from the spoils they took.
CREON. I take it as an omen in our favour.
    You know how we stand, Teiresias. The waves engulf us.
860 The enemy are all around. Thebes is sore pressed.
    Our king has himself gone down to the battlefield
    To face them, and they are strong. But Eteocles

76

Charged me to find out from you
What our best course might be to save the city.
TEIRESIAS. Eteocles? If it's him, my lips are sealed.
  I'll read no oracles for him. But if it's you,
  If you seek enlightenment from me . . . I'll tell you.
  It's diseased, Creon. This city has the plague.
  It's had it ever since the gods were flouted
  And Laius fathered a mate for his own wife
  And Oedipus was brought into this world.
  All that horror of blinding and blood –   870
  It was heaven's warning to Greece.
  Did they think they could cover it up?
  Did his sons think, with time, they'd side-step the gods?
  They hoped to, but they were wrong, the arrogant whelps.
  They despised him, yet they wouldn't let him go.
  They goaded his misery to fury, and he cursed them,
  Out of his torment and shame, he cursed them.
  What did I not do, what did I not tell them?
  And for what? They hated me.
  But death has crept up on them, Creon. It's close.   880
  And they will kill each other.
  And before they have finished – on both sides,
  Dung-heaps of dead.
  And there will be wailing and shrieking in the land,
  And you, O Thebes, no more than a crumbling graveyard.
  Hear me and be warned. Be rid of them,
  All of them. None, no not one, of Oedipus' house
  Must stay here – not as kings, not as meanest citizens.
  They are doom-ridden. They can only wreak havoc.
  And it spreads now. The evil spreads and
  It will overpower you. True, there is
  One resource left you, one hope only,   890
  One way to escape. And yet . . .
  To speak it would not be safe, even for me.
  And for him who could heal all, who holds
  The future of Thebes in his hand – it would be ruin.
  I shall go now. Farewell. I am only one among many.
  I'll endure what may be. What else can I do?

77

CREON. No, Teiresias, don't go.
TEIRESIAS. Take your hand off me.
CREON. Why do you desert us?
TEIRESIAS. Fortune deserts you, not I.
CREON. There's a way to escape, you said so. Tell it to us.
TEIRESIAS. You want me to? You won't want me to, soon

              enough.

900 CREON. I want my city to survive.
TEIRESIAS. You are sure you wish to hear it?
CREON. How could I wish for anything else?
TEIRESIAS. Then I will read the future for you.
 But first I must know one thing. Menoeceus
 Brought me here. Where is he now?
CREON. At your side. Come closer, boy.
TEIRESIAS. No. Tell him to leave us, where
 He cannot hear what I shall reveal.
CREON. He is my son, Teiresias. He will repeat
 Nothing he should not.
TEIRESIAS. You insist that I speak in his presence?
910 CREON. I do. He is eager too to know what may save us.
TEIRESIAS. Hear then the way of prophecy,
 What could be done to save Thebes. .
 You must see Menoeceus here
 Slain for his country's sake. Your son . . .
 Menoeceus . . . You demanded to be told.
CREON. What . . . did you say?
TEIRESIAS. What is ordained. What you have to do.
CREON. You are brief for such a tale of horror.
TEIRESIAS. It may be that for you. It is salvation for your

             country.

CREON. I did not hear it. I was not listening.
 . Thebes can take care of itself.
920 TEIRESIAS. Is that Creon? I don't recognise him.
CREON. Peace be with you, but go now.
TEIRESIAS. This is a frightened man.
CREON. I can do without your divinations!
TEIRESIAS. Is truth destroyed because it distresses you?
CREON. O Teiresias, I clasp your knees, I touch your beard . . .

78

TEIRESIAS. Why kneel to me? The only other way is ruin.
    Do you pray for that?
CREON. Only keep silent. Do not tell this to the city.
TEIRESIAS. That would be wrong. You cannot ask it of me.
    Silence is no longer possible.
CREON. What will you do to me? Will you murder my son?
TEIRESIAS. Others must see to the doing, I only speak.
CREON. But why, Teiresias? Why me and the boy here?
    What happened to bring this horror upon us?
TEIRESIAS. Yes, it is right to ask. You are right to challenge me.   930
    There is a place where the earth asks for blood,
    A deep place in the earth, still demanding a death,
    Which only this boy can give. Long ago
    A dragon dwelled there, guarding the springs of Dirce,
    And it was sacred to the War God. Cadmus killed it,
    And in all these years the god has not forgotten.
    Give him a death for that death, and War becomes
    Your ally. Make that earth rich again. It needs
    Living blood for the blood of life it gave
    When Cadmus sowed it with the dragon's teeth
    And it sent up for him a harvest of armed men   940
    To populate his city. One of that race
    Must pay this death, and of the Dragon Men
    Descended direct, of pure blood on both sides,
    You only – you and your two sons – survive.
    Haemon is exempt, he is not virgin.
    Though his marriage is not solemnised, he is contracted.
    But this boy is as yet pledged only to the city.
    His sacrifice could save it.
    Adrastus would turn home in ruin.   950
    Night would close up Argive eyes.
    Thebes would be made glorious.
    There is your choice. Save which one you will,
    The city or your son. You have all I can tell.
    Take me home, daughter. What's the sense
    In practising my visionary art? A man's future
    Shows disaster, and you're hated for revealing it.
    But if you pity him and lie,

You wrong your sacred calling. The gods
Should do their own interpreting to men.
They have no one to fear.

960 CHORUS. So silent, Creon?
Can you not form the words?
Too shattered for speech, are you?
Yes, I can feel for you.
CREON. What word can there be? No, it is clear
What my word is. I will not rush into ruin.
Offer the city my son's life? Never!
I love him. As any man loves his child.
Who hands his child to death? Who thinks
To slay mine and say that I do well?
It is I who am prepared to die. My life
Makes a fitter and riper sacrifice for Thebes.
970 Menoeceus, make ready, before they all hear of this.
Forget the old man and his mad mumblings.
You must escape, as fast as may be. Fly the country.
He'll go the round of the gates and guard-posts
Telling everyone. If we can forestall him,
You're safe. If not, we're both undone.
It will be your death.
MENOECEUS. Where shall I escape to?
A city somewhere? Or friends?
CREON. Wherever you're furthest from reach of here.
MENOECEUS. Tell me what to do, and I will do it.
CREON. Get beyond Delphi, first . . .
980 MENOECEUS. Yes?
CREON. And into Aetolia . . .
MENOECEUS. Where then?
CREON. Make your way to Thesprotia . . .
MENOECEUS. Where the sacred wood is . . .?
CREON. Where the sacred wood is at Dodona.
MENOECEUS. Will I be safe there?
CREON. You will be under the protection of Zeus there.
He will guide you.
MENOECEUS. How will I provide for myself?

80

CREON. I will see you have money. I will get you some.
MENOECEUS. It is good what you say, father. Hurry then.
  I must go first to your sister, Jocasta,
  And say goodbye to her. She was a mother to me
  When I was orphaned. Then I'll escape.
  But hurry now. You would not delay my going . . .   990

  I did that well. My words were false
  To take away his fear, and win my own way.
  He'd steal me out of here, cheating the city
  Of its only chance, branding me coward,
  Which might be pardonable in someone old
  But would be unforgivable in me.
  Turn traitor to Thebes? No. It gave me birth
  And I will save it. Count on that.
  I am going now to offer up my life,
  To die for my country. Men face death for that
  Who have no prophecies to prompt them.
  They stand unflinching in the ranks of battle
  Fighting for our city, and no fate forces them.   1000
  Shall I then betray my father, brother,
  Thebes itself, and fly like a coward?
  I would not dare such dishonour. Where
  Could I ever live and not be pointed at
  For what I'd done, for all my life?
  O Zeus among the stars, O murderous Ares,
  Who set Earth's harvest of the dragon's teeth
  To be this kingdom's rulers – I am coming.
  My stand will be upon the rampart's top
  High above that deep place in the earth   1010
  The prophet spoke of, which the dragon guarded.
  There I will kill myself and set my country free.
  It is spoken.
  The life I give this city is honourable
  And pure, it will purge her sickness.
  If men would only give, each in his power,
  Their good for the good of all, this world
  Might suffer less, go forward hoping.

CHORAL ODE IV.

Out of an innocent sky came terror
came terror
1020   with a slow flapping of wings,
a thing that was born of darkness
that came up out of the pit
monstrous
to drink Theban blood,
bringing terror
bringing horror –
half woman
but an animal a beast
with wings
circling slow-flapping wings
and claws to tear flesh with.

And one day she appeared suddenly
the Sphinx
out there beyond the river Dirce
and started swooping on children
and carrying them off . . .
That cry that wild bird-scream
that scream as she made her kill
1030   kill kill!
And Thebes whimpered for fear.

What murdering murderous god
ordained such things
allowed such horrors to happen?
Mothers cried out and wept
the young women cried out and wept
homes rang with weeping
cry cry!
weep aloud aloud!
cry one to another through the stricken city!
1040   Grief raging like a storm
a tempest of lamentation
as the winged she-devil

snatched our children
and vanished with another
and another.

Then one day
came striding into Thebes
striding like a hero
with the voices of gods in his head
Oedipus –
fateful Oedipus.
Oh the joy then
the weeping with relief!
It was later the horror came back
when he lay with his mother.
But he was the bright champion
who beat the Sphinx
broke her power
untwisted her riddle.

Yet there had come into the city
something unclean   1050
blood
and a curse
passed on in curses
on his sons
and bitter hate
and strife.

Give thanks
give thanks now
for one who goes to his death
for Thebes' sake
to purify Thebes.
Creon is left to weep
but Thebes is set proud again
in triumph.
Pray for sons as noble   1060
pray that the long curse be lifted.

O Pallas look with favour on us –
you quickened Cadmus' courage
you sped the dragon-slaying rock.
And yet
we have known too long
there is some god
hates us.

Scene Six
The Battle for Thebes

MESSENGER. Ahoy there! Who's guarding the gate?
    Open up, someone. Call out Jocasta. Ahoy there, open!
1070   Come out and hear me, famed wife of Oedipus – this
    Is what you've been waiting for. Leave your wailing and
                                              tears.
JOCASTA. What is it, friend? O friend, what news?
    But no, it is something terrible. It's Eteocles.
    Aren't you his shield-man? Shouldn't you be
    Beside him now, in the battle? Oh, is my son dead?
MESSENGER. If that's your fear, forget it. He's alive.
JOCASTA. How is the city then? Do our defences hold?
MESSENGER. Unbreached as yet. Thebes keeps her honour safe.
1080 JOCASTA. But there was danger?
MESSENGER. Oh, it hung on a knife's edge. But we
    Were the stronger. We Cadmaeans
    With fight inside us can outmatch Mycenae.
JOCASTA. Tell me one thing – what do you know
    Of Polyneices? His life is my care also.
MESSENGER. So far they both survive. Both. So far . . .
JOCASTA. Bless you for that. But how have the Argives
    Been held back? Tell me, so I can go
    To the blind old man in the house and give him glad news.
MESSENGER. There was a sign given to us – a death. It was
1090   Your brother's son, Menoeceus. We caught sight of him
    Standing on the highest tower, saw him thrust his sword
    To the black hilt through his own throat. He gave
    His life for Thebes. That saved us, and the battle turned.

The king your son had posted seven companies,
Picked men and their captains, at the seven gates
To match the Argives, horse and infantry,
Each weighed against the other's with reserves
Ready to rush in wherever the defences weakened.
From the tower-tops we watched them, saw the white shields
Wheel past Teumessus, approach the moat and mass there.   1100
Then they charged, yelling their battle-cry,
And trumpets blared, and back from our own walls
Came the bray of answering trumpets, splitting the air.
First of our seven were the Neistian Gates to bear
The brunt, from a dense horde battering with shields
Brass-bound and spiked, and led by Parthenopaeus
Whose own was blazoned with the sign of Atalanta,
His huntress-mother, shooting the Aetolian Boar.
Against the Gate of Proetus came the warrior-priest,   1110
His chariot laden for the rites of sacrifice,
His shield mute of challenge, his ensign blank.
The Lord Hippomedon attacked the Ogygian Gate
Bearing a shield all eyes for Argus the All-Seeing –
Some opening as the constellations rise,
Some closing when they set, as close they did
When later, death eclipsed his own life's star.
Opposing the next gate – Tydeus: and across his shield   1120
A full-maned lion's pelt, with Prometheus figured
Upon it bearing fire to symbolise
The burning of Thebes. Against the Fountain Gate
Came your son Polyneices, with the fearful sign
On his shield (flexed by pivots against the hand-grip)
Of the mad and maddened flesh-eating Horses of Hades
Running wild. Next Capaneus, whose love of war
Rivals the War God's, led the attack against
The Electran Gate, and stamped out on his shield
With iron studs was one of the Earth Giants,   1130
Bearing a city entire upon his shoulders
Torn up from its foundation – he meant us to know
Our city was destined for no less a fate.
At the last and seventh gate stood Adrastus of Argos.

85

Now close by Argos lived the dreaded serpent
Of the hundred heads, the Hydra, and that was displayed
Upon his shield-arm as if from our Theban walls
It were snatching our Theban men in hungry jaws.
1140   These I saw while taking the password round –
Saw them all clearly as I see you.
The battle began with a rain of arrows and spears
And volleys of sling-shot, and stones crashing down
On all sides. At this stage we were winning,
When there's a shout – 'Sons of the Danaans' . . .
(it was Tydeus and your precious Polyneices)
'What are you waiting for? We'll be strafed to tatters
By this shooting. All together now,
Foot, horse and chariots – charge the gates!'
They heard and were heartened. There was a sudden rally
And bloodied heads began hitting the dust in hundreds –
1150   On our side too, you could see them by dozens
All along the battlements diving to their deaths
And the parched earth turning slippery with blood.
Then Parthenopaeus, Atalanta's son –
He was from Arcadia, not Argos itself –
Came on like a whirlwind up against the gates
Yelling for fire and axes to tear the town apart with.
But he was halted in mid-yell by that son
Of a sea-god, Periclymenus, tumbling a rock down on him
Big as a wagon – just tipped it over
1160   The lip of the parapet, and his gold head cracked open
Like a crushed nut coming apart. One second a face,
The next a purple pulp. *He*'ll not carry
A proud life back to his huntress mother in the mountains.
Well then, Eteocles could see that at this gate
All went well, so on he passed to the next,
With me close behind. And there was Tydeus
With a swarm of his shieldmen, keeping up
Such a barrage of those Aetolian javelins of theirs
Against the topmost tower-face, that men
Were deserting the outer battlements in panic.
Oh, but that son of yours – he could have been a huntsman

86

Whistling up his hounds! He rallied them round again
And packed them back to their posts. So that   1170
Stopped the rot there. And on we hurried to other gates.
Now Capaneus – how can I best describe Capaneus?
He was mad, raging mad. He was way up
One of the tallest scaling-ladders, clinging and climbing,
And how that man ranted! Not Zeus himself,
No, not God's own thunderbolts were going to stop him
Grinding our town to rubble. And all the while
Up he came, jabbering on, stones pelting down on him
Bunched beneath his shield, rung after rounded rung
Up that ladder. He's at the top, head level with the coping   1180
                                                                                                   now
And coming over when – the lightning struck!
There was a deafening crash, the earth shook
And everyone ducked for dear life. And there –
Sailing out from the wall – wheee! like a shot from a sling
Went Capaneus cartwheeling, hair in the wind,
Blood showering down, spinning spread-eagled
Like old Ixion on his wheel.
He was dead when he hit the ground. Burnt out.
A shrivelled cinder.
Well, that convinced Adrastus Zeus wasn't on *his* side
And he smartly pulled his forces back beyond the ditch.
But to us the portent showed heaven was helping
And out we sallied again. Our horse and chariots   1190
Charged. With a solid phalanx of spears
Against their infantry, we smashed into their centre.
It was a massacre. Men cut down and dying,
Slumped across chariot-rails, wheels bucking,
Leaping, axle piled on axle, mounds of dead –
All heaped together in confusion.
So for today at least we've beaten them back,
Our defences have held. It's in the lap of the gods
If Thebes' good fortune lasts, but some god
Surely helped her to survive till now.
CHORUS. Gods looking fair on Thebes may look fair on me.   1200
Shall I not now hope for myself too?

87

JOCASTA. Heaven and fortune both are merciful.
I still have my sons. Our city has escaped.
Only my poor brother, who gave me to Oedipus,
Reaps a harvest of loss. He mourns a son
For whom Thebes must give thanks. Have you more to tell?
What does Eteocles intend?
MESSENGER. The rest can wait. So far all's well and you've been
              lucky.
1210 JOCASTA. What do you mean 'so far'? No, it can't wait.
MESSENGER. What more do you want? Your sons have not been
              killed.
JOCASTA. I need to know if I can trust what's coming.
MESSENGER. I must go. Let me go! I left the King unattended.
JOCASTA. There's something wrong. You're hiding something
              from me.
MESSENGER. I brought you good news. Why should I now tell
              you bad?
JOCASTA. Why should you not sprout wings and fly? Now tell
              me.
MESSENGER. You should have let me leave after the good things.
Why add the rest? All right. Your sons intend –
1220 It's wild, it's wicked of them – to fight it out on their own.
No armies. Single combat. To both sides
They've said it now, and who can unsay it?
Eteocles began it.
He called to the Argive army from high on the ramparts
For silence to let him address them. 'Danaans' he cried,
'You who have come here, captains from the whole
Of Hellas, and you too, people of Thebes,
Why should you sacrifice your lives either
For Polyneices or for me? It is wrong.
I foreswear that sacrifice and will myself
1230 Do battle alone with my brother. If I kill him
I reign alone. If I lose, to him alone
I yield the kingship of Thebes. Abandon this fight,
Men of Argos, leave Thebes in peace, do not die here.
Enough already have died of Cadmus' line.'
He'd hardly finished before your son Polyneices

88

Had leapt to his feet to praise and support what he'd said.
The Argives all cheered their approval, so did we,
For it sounded just. And truce was called there and then,   1240
With both armies' generals meeting out in neutral
Ground between them to swear how solemnly
They'd honour it. Then began the arming
Of the two protagonists, they whose youth
Was acting out their father's ancient doom.
Each had their friends to help them. Limb by limb
They were lapped in bronze, strapped into glittering war-gear,
Thebans aiding the Theban, Argives his brother,
Till both stood forth shining, the hot blood flushing
Their cheeks, each with his own supporters clustering
Round to egg him on, with 'Now, Polyneices,
You can set up your trophy to Zeus, make Argos famed,'   1250
Or 'You are your city's champion, Eteocles,
Conquer and stay king.' And as they urged them on to battle,
Sheep were slain upon altars, and the priests
Began divining what the sacrificial flames
Portended – how many leaping tongues or clefts,
Whether they fizzle with damp (an evil sign)
Or throw up a halo of light (and that could mean
Either thing, a victory or a disaster).
Oh madame, your help is needed. Wise words or prayers,
Magic or spells, anything you can. Hold back your sons   1260
From so awful a struggle. The danger's great.
What grief more than this could you win today
Than both your sons dead . . .?
JOCASTA. Antigone! My daughter! Fetch me my daughter!
  Oh, my innocent girl. This is where childhood
  Ends. The gods are closing in.
  Two marvels of men have told death they're coming,
  And they are blood of your blood.
  But you and I, daughter, are going to stop them,
  You and I both. They must not kill each other.
ANTIGONE. Mother, what is it? Why are you out here?   1270
  I heard a new terror in your voice.
JOCASTA. Your brothers' lives run out.

89

ANTIGONE. I don't understand.

JOCASTA. They are met for single combat.

ANTIGONE. What are you saying?

JOCASTA. Nothing of comfort. Come with me.

ANTIGONE. Where to?

JOCASTA. The battlefield.

ANTIGONE. Oh, mother, how can I? Must I leave this house,
   Must I face those people? They frighten me.

JOCASTA. Come, girl, this is no time for maiden modesty.

ANTIGONE. What . . . am I . . . to do?

JOCASTA. Stop your brothers fighting.

ANTIGONE. I don't know how.

JOCASTA. Do what I do. We'll fall at their feet together.

ANTIGONE. Show me where we go. Let us not lose time.

1280   JOCASTA. Quick then, daughter, quick. Oh, I can live again
   If we forestall them. If not, their death is mine.

CHORAL ODE V.
  Fear . . .
          fear . . .
                  shakes me.
  Over my skin crawls
  pity, pity for that tortured mother.
  Which of her sons will kill her son?

1290   O Zeus, O Earth . . .
  blood-brothers,
  brother's blood,
  which can I weep for?

  Two wolves howling for the kill,
  the rattle of two spears poised for the death-throw,
  and the slow sad stain in the dust.

1300   We can wait only to weep only to cry out,
  even we who are strangers.
  Death is so close.
  Death willed by the Furies.
  The last horror
  for day to reveal.

Hush now, hush. Leave off our tears
And whimpering. Creon is coming.
Poor Creon. The shadow has fallen upon him.

Scene Seven
The Death of the Brothers

CREON. Which am I to weep for first –   1310
  Myself or my city, both like lost souls
  Crossing to the dead shore.
  Look. Here is my son. Sacrificed for Thebes.
  His name will be for ever glorious, but to me
  A never-ending pain. He lay on the Dragon Rocks,
  And I took him in my arms, gathered him, cradled him.
  There is a cry goes up from all my house.
  I have grown old. I come to seek comfort of the old.
  Where is my sister, the Queen, Jocasta, to lay out
  My dead son? The dead must have their due
  From us who are old but still not dead.   1320
  The gods below must have their due.
CHORUS. Jocasta has gone, Creon. Antigone with her.
CREON. Gone? Gone where? And why have they gone?
CHORUS. She heard her sons were to fight it out –
  Who would be king – in single combat.
CREON. What are you telling me? I did not know,
  I did not know this too . . . I had my son . . .
CHORUS. And time has passed now since her leaving.
  The fight could be ended . . .   1330
CREON. Must I bear this also, the sign approaching
  That it is true? A man comes running
  With news. And fate in his eyes . . .
MESSENGER. Oh God, how am I to tell what I have to tell?
  I bring a burden of grief, nothing but grief.
CREON. We know grief already. What would you tell?
MESSENGER. Oh, Creon, your sister's sons are dead.
CREON. Do you hear that, house of Oedipus?   1340
  You too! Your sons too are dead!
CHORUS. Would the walls themselves not weep

91

Did they but know?

MESSENGER. And to that sorrow add sorrow.

CREON. Have you more?

MESSENGER. Your sister died with her sons.

CHORUS. Ahee!

1350   Wail, howl, beat the head in mourning!

CREON. Jocasta, O Jocasta, O my sister . . .
    That it should all end here and all the curse
    Come true. What happened to them?

MESSENGER. It had gone so well. You know how we beat back
    The attack on the towers. From the walls there, you could see
                                              it.

1360   But then the brothers, resplendent in full armour,
    Had come out together into the dead ground
    Between the armies, ready to fight it out alone.
    And Polyneices looked towards Argos
    And called on the Queen of Heaven . . .
    'Dread Hera, I am thine now,
    Thine since I wed the daughter of Adrastus
    And dwell in his land. Grant me
    To kill this brother. Grant that my hand
    Signal its victory, stained with my foe's blood.'
    It was so terrible a prayer, so awful the trap

1370   Which fate had caught them in, that many felt tears,
    And in that watching crowd, glances met
    As if in shame, and had to look away.
    But Eteocles was looking towards Thebes, his home,
    And he called on Athene of the golden shield –
    'Daughter of Zeus, guide thou my hand. Let victory
    Sit on my spear. Let this arm loose it at my brother's breast
    And kill him who came here to lay my country waste.'
    It was like a beacon-blaze to signal the fight.
    A trumpet blared and they sprang at each other

1380   As if they were wild boars whetting their savage tusks
    And slavering at the mouth. They jockeyed
    For position, spears poised and quivering, but each
    Kept crouched within the circle of his shield,
    Offering no target. But if one saw the other's eye

Peer round the rim, in went the spear then
With a quick stab, quick jab, to get past his guard.
But they were both too cunning, using the eye-squints
In their shields. So, for a time, spears could do nothing.
And we, watching, waited and sweated,
Fearful, the lot of us, more than the fighters
We sweated for. Suddenly Eteocles flicked his foot,   1390
Scuffing a stone aside, and his leg showed
Out beyond the edge of his shield.
Polyneices saw it and struck,
Aimed straight for the hostage offered to his spear
And sliced the blade of it clean through his calf.
Up went a roar of applause from the whole Argive army.
But in lunging he'd exposed his shoulder
And Eteocles, wounded though he was, saw that and caught

                            him

A blow between the ribs that staggered him,
So that the Thebans cheered in their turn.
But the spearhead broke, and with his weapon useless,   1400
He fell back a step or two, caught up a jagged stone,
Hurled it, and snapped the other's spear-shaft
Clean in two. They were evenly matched again,
Both without spears. Instantly two hands
Snatched for their swords. They closed and locked
With a crash of shields that rocked the ground.
But Eteocles had a trick he'd learned in Thessaly
And now he used it. As they heaved and grappled
He suddenly gave way, throwing his weight
Back on the left foot, but keeping his eye   1410
Watchful for the hollow of the man's belly opposite,
Then lunged on the right foot, forward, shot
The blade through his navel and felt it jar in the spine.
Polyneices in an agony doubled up, chest
Over stomach, and choking in blood, collapsed.
And Eteocles, victorious, exultant,
Stuck his sword in the ground and bent
To strip him of his arms, conscious
Only of that, not of himself.

And that was his undoing. For Polyneices,
With still a gasp left in him, had even in his agony
1420 Clung to his sword as he fell, and with a last convulsion
Reached up and sank it in Eteocles' bowels.
They lie there, the two of them, close beside each other,
With dust in their teeth, and no certain victory.
CHORUS. Weep yet for Oedipus, the grief of Oedipus –
Oh dark, blind king, your curse was heard and heeded.
MESSENGER. Hear now the grief that followed.
For where her sons were fallen and were dying,
1430 Came their mother running in anxious haste,
She and her daughter, saw the wounds,
Saw their death upon them,
And cried out for her sons and her vain help.
She threw herself down, she fell by each in turn,
She wailed, she wept her wasted love,
And by her all the while, like one
Who shielded her, their sister crying
To those so dear, those who left helpless now
Mother and unwed maid.
And Eteocles battled for breath, but forced
One dying gasp. For he could hear his mother
And stretched out an ice-cold hand to touch her.
1440 But no voice came. His eyes spoke only,
And tears to tell her his love.
But his brother was breathing yet, and
Gazed on Antigone and on his aged mother –
'We are lost, my mother. I weep for you,
And you, my sister. And for my brother dead.
Yes, I loved him. We became enemies,
But I did love him. Oh mother, bury me –
And you, my sister – here in my own land.
1450 I lost our house, but they will not deny me
That much of my native soil? You will
Persuade them? Mother . . . close my eyes . . .'
And he laid her hand over them, 'Farewell . . .
The dark is closing round . . .'
So both sad lives together ended on a breath.

And when their mother saw it, saw that the whole disaster
Was wound up, all her pent suffering spilled over
In one last, fearful act. She snatched a sword up
From the dead and thrust it through her throat.
So she lies now with those she loved,
Her arms in a last embrace about them both.
Almost at once a fierce dispute broke out   1460
Between the armies, Thebes shouting that our king
Had won, they Polyneices. Captains railed
At one another – was it not Polyneices' spear
Struck first? No, how can dead men claim a victory?
And none had noticed Antigone steal away . . .
Then the Argives rushed to arms, but we –
And well for us that we had made provision –
Had never laid ours aside. We fell upon them
Before their defence was ready, struck hard
Without warning along the whole army's length.
There was none could stop us. Men pelting for their lives   1470
Poured out across the plain, and blood
Gathered into pools where dead men lay
With spears in their backs. And so we beat them.
The battle trophies are going up already
To Zeus the Victorious. They're stripping the killed
Of their shields, and spoils are being sent
Into the city. But some even now
Make their way here, bringing Antigone
And her dead for us to mourn.
The battle is over, but for Thebes
That is a joy with no joy in it.

Scene Eight
Oedipus

CHORUS. Now no longer the words only,   1480
   No longer the troubled tongue telling of it.
   Here comes grief itself into your midst
   For you to see –
   Three dead brought here before the house,

95

Three who took their way together
Into the trackless dark.
ANTIGONE. Tear off the veil now,
No shame, no modesty,
No hiding the hot blood, the hot tears,
No shrinking from this death . . .
Take me in the dance, Dionysus,
I give myself to you dancing.
1490 Strip this band from my hair,
Untie the knot of my robe,
I bring you the dead in the triumph of despair.
Ahee!
O my brother, your fate and Thebes' fate
Spelled out together in that name of yours –
The dread design accomplished,
The house of Oedipus destroyed.
Your fretful striving was no striving,
But death given for death
In desolation and terror,
Lifeblood for lifeblood . . .
Come my city, my home,
Who will sing the lament with me,
1500 And add their tears,
And add their tears?
What singer can I call to join me
Who bring three, blood of my blood,
Slaughtered mother and sons?
Do you laugh to see them, you Furies,
Are you satisfied at last
Who have hounded our house,
Worked ruin for all the line of Oedipus,
Ever since that hour he caught out the Sphinx
In her riddle and stopped
The song dead in her throat?
O my father –
Who of all Greece, who
1510 Of all the noblest princes of this world
Ever in their brief day suffered

What you have suffered
With all men's eyes upon you . . .!
And I too am left desolate
To sing ever my song alone.
Not the bird that sits in the oak tree
Or perches in the high branch of the olive
Can match my mourning note,
Nor aid my sorrow.
For my mother is gone from me
And lonely the life I am left,   1520
Lonely the tears, the tears . . .
See, I tear my hair,
I lay it on the dead, an offering –
Which first?
On the dear dry breasts of my mother
Which gave me suck,
Or the gaping death-wounds
Of my brothers?
Ahee!
Father, O my father, come out!   1530
You are weary, old now and weary,
Groping your way endlessly round and round
That blind cage you made for yourself,
Dragging the weight of your life
Through that sleepless fog.
But now you must leave it,
Old Oedipus,
You must bring your ravaged, blinded face
Out here,
Into the light.

OEDIPUS. What do you want with me, girl,
Here in the open? My staff! My feet cannot see!
What right have your tears to drag me   1540
From my bed in the dark? I am only
A grey ghost of a thing,
A shadowless dead thing,
I do not belong out here
In this waking world.

ANTIGONE. You have got to know what has happened,
 What *is* out here.
 Your sons are dead, Oedipus.
 And your wife is dead who loved you,
 And was your staff and cared for you,
1550 And cherished your blind age.
OEDIPUS. Oh spare me, spare me more suffering!
 Three gone together? How, child, how?
ANTIGONE. Your curse – no, father, no blame,
 No reproaches, I weep for it like you –
 But it fell on your sons and crushed them,
 A fire that consumed them, a sword
 That cut them to pieces.
OEDIPUS. Oh my children! Ahee . . .!
1560 ANTIGONE. Yes, cry for them! Oh, had you eyes now
 To see the bright sun galloping overhead
 And here below, the bodies of the slain!
OEDIPUS. Their fate, my sons . . . I understand.
 But what of my wife?
ANTIGONE. She went down to them, went down
 To plead with them, plead with them
 In front of them all, crying out
 And weeping and baring her mother's breasts.
1570 It was just past Electra's Gate she found them,
 Where the meadow is thick with flowers,
 Fighting to the death like caged lions
 Clawing at each other's wounds.
 But their lives had drained from them already.
 War had poured its libation to Death.
 And she took from the cold hand its bronze-hammered sword
 And turned it on herself, despairing.
 She died embracing them. Oh, father,
1580 All in one day whatever power
 Spells out our fate has heaped the woes
 Of our house in one black woe together.
CHORUS. A day that brings disaster on Oedipus
 And all his line. O, lighten humanity's load!

98

CREON. It is time to leave mourning. The dead
  Call for burial. Oedipus, listen
  To what I must tell you now. Eteocles,
  Your son, appointed me his heir
  Here in Thebes. It was to be his dowry
  For Antigone's marriage to my son, Haemon.
  I cannot, for the sake of Thebes, permit you
  To live here longer. Teiresias said it plainly –   1590
  While you remain, Thebes cannot be well.
  You must go. I do not say this
  For your hurt. I am not your enemy.
  I simply fear the curse that follows you
  And the harm it could yet do us.
OEDIPUS. O fate, have you not from my beginning
  Bred me wretched beyond all men,
  Singled me out for suffering? My mother
  Had not laboured yet to bring me to the light
  Before Apollo told how I, unborn,
  Should kill my father, and he, my begetter,   1600
  Knew me as his destined death, tried to destroy me,
  Tore me from my mother's breast and threw me
  To the mercy of wild beasts on the bleak
  Mountain side. But I was saved.
  Saved! O you place of desolation,
  Why were you not sunk fathoms deep
  In hell for not destroying me?
  You let me go, let me be rescued,
  Cared for at Polybus' court, lovingly
  Led towards the horror of
  My fate's fulfilment. I killed my father,
  Bedded with my mother, got on her sons
  Who were my brothers, and whom I now   1610
  Have killed, passing to them
  The curse that Laius laid on me.
  What does heaven want of me?
  I was not born mad! Never could I
  Have done such things of my own nature,
  Against my eyes, against my sons,

If the whole cruel, senseless cycle
Had not been god-contrived against me!
Ah well, it's done. What do I do now
With this wasted shell? Who is to guide
The blind old man? She who's dead?
Were she alive she would, I know.
Or my fine sons? I do not have any.
Am I young enough still to earn my own bread?

1620   How? Creon, why slay me utterly?
For you do slay me if you cast me out.
But I'll not beg from you. I'll not
Go down on my knees to you. Wronged
I may be. I'll not demean my birth.

CREON. No, you must not kneel to me.
But I, too, cannot let you stay among us.
As to these two dead brothers, one
Must be taken now into the palace. The other,
Polyneices, for siding with our enemies
Against the safety of the state, is to be thrown out

1630   Beyond the city's boundaries and left
Unburied. This proclamation to Thebes –
'Any attempt to honour this corpse,
Lay wreaths on it or cover it with earth,
Will be punished with death. It is to be left
Unattended, unwept, for kites and vultures.'
Come, Antigone. We understand
Your distress, your triple loss.
Compose yourself now. Come indoors. The city
Grieves with you, but tomorrow you'll make Thebes
Rejoice again when Haemon and you are married.

ANTIGONE. Oh, father, this makes your wretchedness perfect.

1640   I could pity you even more than the dead,
Griefs crowd upon you unalloyed.
Creon, if you are to be the new authority
In Thebes, how can you wrong him so
And reject him so and make these barbarous
Decrees against the defenceless dead?

CREON. That decision was Eteocles', not mine.

100

ANTIGONE. It is still senseless, and you a fool to follow it.
CREON. I am executing what the King enjoined
  Upon me. That is right and proper.
ANTIGONE. It's wicked. He decreed it out of malice and hate.
CREON. Throwing that one to the dogs is natural justice.   1650
ANTIGONE. It's not. It's revenge. And it's against the law.
CREON. Polyneices was a traitor to Thebes.
ANTIGONE. For that he has already forfeited his life.
CREON. And right to burial.
ANTIGONE. Why? He claimed the share of his own country
  Which was due him. Where was the sin in that?
CREON. Antigone, he will not be granted burial.
ANTIGONE. Then I will bury him, whatever the state says.
CREON. You will bury yourself beside him.
ANTIGONE. Why not? We loved each other. That would be
                                       beautiful
  And right, to lie together.
CREON. Restrain her, someone. Take her indoors.   1660
ANTIGONE. Take your hands off! I'll not let go of him.
CREON. This is sacrilege, girl. It's not for you to decide.
ANTIGONE. 'Thou shalt not outrage the dead.' Who decides
                                         that?
CREON. No one is to cover that body.
ANTIGONE. For his mother's sake, Creon, for Jocasta's sake . . .
CREON. You are wasting your time.
ANTIGONE. Let me wash him, let me only . . .
CREON. It has been expressly forbidden . . .
ANTIGONE. Bind up those hideous wounds . . .
CREON. To tend his body in any way.   1670
ANTIGONE. Beloved, at least on your dear lips, one kiss.
CREON. You desecrate your marriage!
ANTIGONE. Do you think I would live to wed your son?
CREON. You must. What else can you do? Where else can you
                                         go?
ANTIGONE. If you force me to it, I'll kill him.
CREON. You hear that, Oedipus? She'll say anything.
  She abuses us all.
ANTIGONE. I swear it. By this sword of my brother's, I swear it.

CREON. Why, girl, is such a marriage
  So impossible for you?
ANTIGONE. I am going with my father. I will share
  His exile and his misery.
1680 CREON. That is generous in you. It is noble.
  But I cannot think it wise.
ANTIGONE. I will stay with him till death, and die with him.
CREON. Go, then. Go. Let my son be safe from you.
  Go with your father. Leave us. Leave Thebes.

OEDIPUS. He may not praise your spirit, child.
  I do. And your love.
ANTIGONE. How could I marry and see you go into exile alone?
OEDIPUS. Stay and be happy. I can bear my ills.
ANTIGONE. You are blind. Who would take care of you?
OEDIPUS. I'll go as fate guides me. Where I fall, I fall.
ANTIGONE. Ah, where is Oedipus now? And the famous riddle?
OEDIPUS. Gone. One day for glory, one to be destroyed.
1690 ANTIGONE. I must share in that.
OEDIPUS. You would share the shame.
ANTIGONE. Not shame, father. Honour.
OEDIPUS. Take my hand. Now guide me
  To where I can touch your mother.
ANTIGONE. Here. This is she.
OEDIPUS. O my unhappy wife . . . Mother, my mother . . .
ANTIGONE. All sorrows met in her.
OEDIPUS. Where do my sons lie?
ANTIGONE. Here. Side by side.
OEDIPUS. Lay my unseeing hand upon their faces.
1700 ANTIGONE. Now you are touching them.
OEDIPUS. O dear dead sons, as pitiable as your father . . .
ANTIGONE. O Polyneices, doubly dear to me . . .
OEDIPUS. It works to its end now. The last
  Of all that was foretold.
ANTIGONE. More yet was foretold?
OEDIPUS. I shall die in exile. On Athenian soil.
ANTIGONE. Attica will take you in? Where?
OEDIPUS. It is a hallowed place. Where the Holy Horseman
                                        dwells.

102

Called Colonus. Come, girl, you have chosen
To share the lot of your blind father.
Guide me on my way.

ANTIGONE. Give me your hand. I help you   1710
As the wind helps on the ship.

OEDIPUS. So, I set out. You and I together, child.
Now your trial begins.

ANTIGONE. My trial. Yes. Mine is the hardest trial
Of all the daughters of Thebes.

OEDIPUS. Where do we go? Reach me my staff.

ANTIGONE. This way, this way, with me.   1720
Like this, like this, your feet.
Your strength is like a dream.

OEDIPUS. Look at me, you who disown me!
An old man shamefully, pitifully hounded
From my home. O God, what I am made to suffer!

ANTIGONE. You suffer? You suffer? O, father, others
Have suffered too, because of a blindness before
You blinded yourself.

OEDIPUS. My name was sung to heaven. Was it blindness
To have seen into the Sphinx's riddle   1730
And guessed it and saved Thebes?

ANTIGONE. That is dead, father, it is forgotten.
It is no longer a glory.
Don't pride yourself now on what is past.
Always for you there has been waiting
This last anguish,
To wander the wilderness and, somewhere,
To die far from home.
But I leave a home where friends
Grew with me from girlhood,
And I weep tears of longing for them.
I go from my land a fugitive
From all my sex. That is my wilderness.

OEDIPUS. And a true heart is your fate.   1740

ANTIGONE. It may earn me a remembrance
As sad as my father's.
My fate is bound also to yours, my brother,

103

So wronged in death, abandoned and unburied.
I may die for it, father, but secretly tonight
I'll bury him. I must.

OEDIPUS. Go back to your friends.

ANTIGONE. They have shared my grief enough.

OEDIPUS. At the altars of the gods . . .

1750 ANTIGONE. I have wearied them with prayers.

OEDIPUS. Seek refuge at least in Dionysus. His holy place
Is in the hills, unknown to all but those
Who worship him.

ANTIGONE. Yes, there was a time I knew him.
I wore the fawnskin too with other Theban maids,
I danced the hills in Semele's sacred throng.
Not now. What can I offer him now?
I no longer have that homage in my heart.

OEDIPUS. Mark me, you Thebans! I am Oedipus –
Oedipus who read the famous riddle,
Who was the greatest among you.
Oedipus, who was the only one

1760 Could break the Sphinx's murderous hold on you
And did it alone! Look at me now!
Disowned, dishonoured. Fit only to be pitied.
And yet . . . pity's no use. Grieving's no use.
The gods decree and we are mortal.
There's no appeal.
We must bear it.

CHORUS. O sacred crown of life –
To win through!
Reward me and
Stay with me
To the end.

BACCHAE

Translated by J. Michael Walton

Characters

DIONYSOS, *son of Zeus and Semele*
TEIRESIAS, *a prophet*
KADMOS, *founder and former King of Thebes*
PENTHEUS, *his grandson, now King*
SERVANT
FIRST MESSENGER
SECOND MESSENGER
AGAUË, *mother of Pentheus*
ATTENDANTS
CHORUS OF ASIAN BACCHAE

Before the palace of Thebes. Enter DIONYSOS.

DIONYSOS. Here am I, Dionysos.
  Son of Zeus and Kadmos' daughter, Semele.
  I have returned to this land of Thebes
  Where I was born from the lightning bolt.
  Now I stand by the springs of Dirke and the waters of
                                        Ismenos,
  A god . . . disguised as a man.
  By the palace I see my mother's memorial,
  Smouldering with the deathless fire of Zeus,
  My mother who proved only too mortal
  Faced by Hera's unrelenting spite.
  Kadmos is my grandfather. I admire him.   10
  He had his tomb erected on hallowed ground.
  I had it wreathed with vine-leaves in profusion.
  I have left behind the gold-rich lands of Lydia and Phrygia,
  Deserted the sun-parched shore of Persia,
  The Baktrian fortress and the cruel land of the Mede.
  Through Arabia I came, prosperous Arabia,
  And through all of Asia where Greeks and foreigners
  Mix in the lofty cities by the shore.
  Now I have come to Greece, this city first.   20
  The dances and ceremonies invented across the sea
  To celebrate my godhead, I now bring here.
  Here, in Thebes, I have first excited women's cries –
  These women of Thebes, the first to dress in fawnskin –
  Placed in their hands my thyrsos, the ivy-covered shaft.
  Why these? Because these sisters of my mother,
  These aunts of mine, denied that I was born of Zeus.
  The last who should have done so, they defamed my
                                mother,
  Semele, proclaiming my god-like birth a trick
  Devised by Kadmos to save a harlot-daughter's face.   30
  That was why, they said, Zeus incinerated my mother,

For her presumption. I have driven them mad.
Homes abandoned, they roam the mountains,
Out of their senses, deranged: every last woman in
                                        Thebes,
Up there amongst the rocks and the trees,
Witless and homeless, Kadmos' daughters too.
40   Thebes will have to learn to appreciate me
And my rituals. My mother will receive her recognition
When all acknowledge my divinity.
Kadmos has grown old and abdicated his throne
To his grandson Pentheus. This Pentheus wages holy war
On me, offers no libations, ignores me in his prayers.
I am going to have to show this Pentheus, show all of
                                        Thebes,
50   What kind of god I am. And when I have succeeded,
I shall move on. But if Thebes takes it in mind to resist
And tries to drive my Bacchants from the mountains,
Then I must lead my women as their general.
Which is why you see me now in human form.

Come now my women, come now my dears.
This is not Tmolos, you're no longer in Lydia.
Come now my acolytes, my fawnskin fawners,
Drawn from far places, eager to serve me.
Rattle your castanets, clatter your drums,
Cymbals and tambours of Rhea, the great Mother.
60   Clash them and strike them. Batter the palace,
Din down on Pentheus. The city must witness.
While I to the mountains depart by myself,
There to accompany the mad Mainad dances.
Exit DIONYSOS. Enter CHORUS.
CHORUS. Far from Asia, land of Asia,
  I have come and I cry,
  I have come and I praise,
  I laud the name of Bromios,
  Dionysos.
  I praise his name, I laud his name,
  Toil but a sweet toil,
  The burden sweet as we praise his holy name.
  Bacchios. Dionysos.

110

Where? What? Who can resist us?
Who on the road? Who in the doorway?
Beware. Let them beware.   70
Let them stand aside, say nothing, stay dumb.
One name we cry. Let none say another.
Dionysos.

Happy. Happy is the one. Blessed is the one
Who comes to know the mysteries,
The mysteries of the gods,
Who hallows life, who yields.
Who yields, lets the soul dance.
Pure is our dance in the mountains,
Purified the dancer in the name of Dionysos.
Sacred are the rites, secret rites for Kybele, the Mother.
Break through, yield. Break through, yield.   80
Break through with thyrsos aloft.
Serve him, serve Dionysos.
Come, Bacchants, come.
Dionysos is your god, god son of god.
Escort him home, home from Phrygia,
Home to Greece, the broad streets of Greece.
Bring him home, your Dionysos.

Dionysos god. Mother labours.
Lightning flashes. Zeus destroys, but Zeus preserves.   90
Mother dies, but Zeus preserves.
Preserved from the fire, concealed in his thigh,
Fastened there with golden pin,
All too quick for jealous Hera's eye.
In due time, as Fate decrees,
He is born, but what a child,   100
What a child from Zeus' thigh.
A savage child with horns and serpents in his hair.
His Mainads wear them still,
The child, Dionysos.

Thebes, city of Semele, Semele's nurse,
Crown her with ivy, crown her with fir,
Crown her with evergreen, berry and flower.

111

110 Brandish the thyrsos, twine wool through the fawn.
Then free her to dance
In the name of our god.
Free from the shuttle,
Free from the loom,
She waits for her leader,
Possessed by the god,
Dionysos.

120 And Krete with its deep holy birthplace of Zeus,
Krete where the Korybants first beat the drum,
Drummed and mixed drumming with Phrygian flute,
The sweet thunder from which they offered to Rhea,
A gift which she used as the true Bacchic note.
130 From her it was raped by the satyrs' mad band,
Who created a dance for the god they adore,
Dionysos.

Sweet, sweet it is to run through the hills.
Sweet to wear the fawnskin.
Sweet to fall enraptured.
Sweet is the hunt, sweet the goat,
140 Sweet the taste, sweet the raw blood.
To run through the hills, through Phrygia, sweet,
To follow through Lydia the lead of our god,
Dionysos.
The earth flows with milk, the earth flows with wine,
With honey it flows.
The smoke like incense from brandished brand.

Run, shout, scream and cry.
150 Dance and fly,
Hair streaming behind.
On Bacchae, on Bacchae.
Far from Tmolos,
Golden Tmolos,
Praise him, praise him,
Praise his godhead.
160 Sacred song
And sacred dance,

112

Mountain high and mountain wide,
Deepest drum and shrillest pipe,
Celebrate his furious flight.
Dionysos.
Enter TEIRESIAS.

TEIRESIAS. Gatekeeper. Are you there?   170
Call Kadmos, son of Agenor
Who left Sidonia to fortify this place.
What's keeping you?
Tell him Teiresias wants him.
He knows why I'm here. We made a bargain,
One old man to his elder,
To dress up in fawnskins, thyrsos in hand
And wreaths about our brows.
Enter KADMOS.

KADMOS. I thought it must be you, old friend.   180
I heard your voice indoors. Sound words from a sound
                                              man.
Here I am, fit and ready, all dressed up
As the god requires. After all, he is my daughter's boy,
Dionysos, revealed to man as a god,
And we must do our best by him.
Where should we go and dance, do you think,
Shaking a leg, an aged head if it comes to that?
You'd better lead, Teiresias. We are neither of us
As young as we were, but you're the clever one.
I feel I could dance day and night, non-stop,
Beating the ground with my thyrsos;
And never a thought to age.

TEIRESIAS. I share your enthusiasm. I feel young and I shall
                                              dance. 190
KADMOS. Excellent. Let's order my chariot to take us to the
                                              mountains.
TEIRESIAS. No chariot. We would dishonour the god.
KADMOS. No chariot. I'll help you, then, one old man with
                                              another.
TEIRESIAS. We'll never weary. The god will be leading us.
KADMOS. Will we be the only men dancing for Bacchios?

113

TEIRESIAS. We alone are in our right minds. No one else.
KADMOS. We may as well get moving, then. Take my hand.
TEIRESIAS. Where are you? Ah, there. Now, don't let go.
KADMOS. I'm only a man, not one to scorn a god.
200 TEIRESIAS. It is not for us to reason about the gods.
   We hold what our fathers held,
   And their fathers before them, from time immemorial.
   They didn't waste time rationalising
   And philosophising. Suppose someone says
   I look a fool at my age going off to dance
   With ivy in my hair, it is no shame to me.
   The god has decreed that we should dance,
   Young and old, and dance I shall.
   No half measures for this god. No one is exempt.
210 KADMOS. Being blind you will not have seen, Teiresias,
   So I'd better warn you. Here's Pentheus in a hurry,
   My grandson to whom I abdicated.
   He looks rather cross. Bad news, perhaps.
   Enter PENTHEUS attended.
   PENTHEUS. I only have to leave town,
   Go away for a few days and what happens?
   What's this I hear about strange goings-on,
   Women leaving home to roam around the mountains,
   Prancing through the trees in honour of this fashionable
                                                         god,
220   Dionysos, whoever he may be?
   And, of course, in the midst of all this revelry,
   Drink. Then off they creep to bed down
   With some man in a quiet corner. Dionysos?
   It's the goddess of lust they're celebrating.
   I've caught some of them, chained them up.
   There they stay in the public prison.
   As for the rest, Ino is among them,
   Aktaion's mother Autonoë, and even Agauë
230   Who bore me to my father Echion.
   I will hunt them down,
   And when I have them safe under lock and key,
   I'll put a stop to this Bacchic nonsense.

114

I hear too that some foreigner has turned up,
Some juggling charmer from Lydia,
All golden hair and perfume,
Flushed with drink and oh so beautiful.
It's he debauches them night and day.
When I get my hands on him,
I'll stop him swinging his twig.   240
I'll part his head from his neck.
He's the one who claims Dionysos is a god,
Who was sewn in Zeus' thigh,
When we know perfectly well the mother
Was blasted together with the child
For claiming Zeus as her lover.
The nerve of him. I don't care who he is.
Hanging's too good for him.

Oh, here's another marvel.
Teiresias the prophet, all dolled-up in a fawnskin.   250
And my grandfather too.
How ridiculous he looks with that stick.
Dear old man, I hate to see you so witless.
Take off the ivy. Please. Give me the thyrsos.
Grandfather, please. This is your fault, Teiresias.
It suits you to introduce some new god,
So you can pocket a commission.
If your senility did not protect you,
I would lock you up with the women for introducing
These foul practices. It's always the same.   260
The moment you allow drink at a women's festival,
Things turn unhealthy.
CHORUS. Profanity. Profanity.
Strange man, have you no respect?
Respect for Kadmos, sower of the earth-born, dragon-
                                                                   spawn?
As Echion's son, do you scorn your own house?
TEIRESIAS. A wise man with a good cause finds eloquence
                                                                    easy.
You talk well enough but there's no sense in your words.
Bold you may be, and capable too,   270

115

But, without sense, a man like you is a public liability.
He is new, perhaps, this god whom you mock . . .
But I cannot begin to tell you how great his influence
Will one day be throughout Greece.
You are a young man. Listen to what I say.
There are two main principles in human experience,
Just two. The first is Demeter,
Mother Earth, whatever you care to call her.
She nurtures us humans by the gift of solid food.
Then there's Semele's son who discovered wine,
A liquid to match her mortal gift with his,
A gift to soothe the troubled mind

280   And bring us restful sleep, the best of all remedies.
We pour libations so that he, a god,
May benefit from mankind.
Oh, you make fun, do you, of that stuff
About Zeus' thigh, and the baby sewn up in it?
Let me tell you the truth about that.
It's just a story, a beautiful story.
When Zeus rescued Dionysos from the ashes,
After the lightning-bolt, he carried the baby away to
                              Olympos.
Hera wanted to throw the god-like child out of heaven.

290   Zeus, with all a god's cunning, concocted this plan.
Out of the ethereal layer which surrounds the earth,
He constructed a surrogate, a phantom child
Which he gave to Hera, thus protecting
The real Dionysos from his wife's anger.
But in time men confused 'ethereal layer'
With 'laid in the thigh', a simple error of transmission.
So myths are made.

Another thing you should consider
Is that Dionysos is a god of prophecy.
Bacchants, like madmen, have method. When the god
Invades a man, that man can see the future.

300   Or you could find Dionysos in the field of Ares,
God of war. Have you never heard of soldiers
Drawn up under arms, stricken with panic

Before they can lift a spear?
That is the 'madness' of Dionysos.
It's Dionysos you can see
Hurtling over the rocks at Delphi,
Hair streaming, wand shaking,
His powers already formidable in Greece.

Pentheus, listen.   310
Do not be so proud as to think that brute force
Is all that makes a man strong.
Only a diseased mind sees power as physical strength.
Accept this god in your kingdom, reverence him,
Crown him, worship him, in his particular way.

As for the women, Dionysos does not require chastity,
But a temperate mind controls any circumstance.
Take note of that. The Bacchic rites alone
Never lead to corruption.
You know yourself what a joy it is to stand at your gates
Before a cheering multitude. No harm in that.
Allow him, then, his due, the respect which pleases him.   320
Kadmos and I, decked out in our finery,
We will dance for him. An aged pair but,
Mock if you must, we will dance.
Nothing you can say will make us oppose a god.
It is you, alas, who have lost your sanity,
Sick beyond any drugs to cure.

CHORUS. Wise words, old man. Apollo could not grudge
    Your reverence for Dionysos, a mighty god.

KADMOS. My boy, I tell you, Teiresias offers good advice.   330
    Become one of us. Do as we do.
    Your head's in the clouds. Think again.
    There is this too. Even if this god is not really a god,
    As you believe, you could at least say that he is.
    It's just a little white lie. Semele gives birth to a god,
    And our family gets the credit.
    You saw what happened to your cousin Aktaion,
    Torn to pieces by the man-eating hounds he'd reared.
    And you know why he suffered.

117

340   All for claiming he was better than Artemis at hunting.
    May you never suffer like that.
    Come, let me crown you with ivy.
    Join us in honouring the god.
    PENTHEUS. Leave me alone. Go on. Dance about, if you must.
    I want none of this foolishness.
    But the man who taught you this folly,
    He shall get what he deserves.
    Go immediately to his seat of prophecy,
    And uproot it. Use crowbars if you have to.
350   Leave nothing standing.
    Throw all his trumpery to the winds.
    Perhaps then he'll take me seriously.
    The rest of you, search the city.
    I want him found, this freak who infects our women,
    Corrupting our beds. And when you catch him,
    Tie him up and bring him here.
    We'll see how he dances when it's raining stones.
    Exit PENTHEUS.
    TEIRESIAS. Oh, you fool, you do not realise what you are
                                    saying.
    Witless before, you're now stark mad.
360   Kadmos, we must go, do what we can for the man,
    However brutish his behaviour:
    Do what we can for our city, god preserve it.
    Pick up your staff and follow me. Help prop me up,
    And I'll support you. It would be shaming
    For a pair of old men to fall over. Still we must go.
    Son of Zeus, Dionysos must be served.
    Pentheus' name means grief. That is no prophecy,
    Kadmos. It is a fact. A foolish man. Foolish words.
    May he never bring grief upon your house.
    Exeunt TEIRESIAS *and* KADMOS.
370   CHORUS. Reverence, queen of gods,
    Flying, gold-winged, over man.
    Reverence, do you realise,
    Did you hear what Pentheus said?
    Do you hear how he slights,

How he sneers at the name of Dionysos?
Dionysos is Semele's son, blessed and crowned,
Lord of the dance and lord of laughter,   380
Redeemer from care at the feast of the vine,
And when the wine's drunk and the festival over
He delivers the ivy-clad Bacchants to sleep.

What is the result of an unbridled tongue,
What is the end of lawless misjudgement?
The outcome disaster, only disaster.
A life lived in quiet, a life tranquil and sane,
Preserves the house and keeps it from harm.   390
The gods, far off, still gaze upon mortals.
Overstepping the mark is simply fool's wisdom,
Gaining him nothing who chases too far.
This way lies madness, attempting the summit,   400
Ill-judged and ill-starred, crashing to earth.

Let me come, let me come, to Aphrodite's isle,
To fairest Kypros where love's charms are fashioned.
There hundred-tongued the rivers give richness
To land untouched by rain.
Or let me come to Pieria,
Lovely Pieria where the Muses live,   410
To the slopes of Olympos, the holy.
Bromios, Dionysos, lead me there, dancing god.
There to the home of Desire and the Graces.
Lead me where dancing to Bacchios is welcome.

Our lord, son of Zeus, delights in the feast.
One goddess I name who pleases him more.
Giver of comfort, giver of joy,
Allowing young men to relish their youth.
The goddess he loves is the goddess of Peace.   420
To rich and to poor he brings gifts of enchantment,
Gifts he bestows through the virtue of wine.
But the man who declines, by day or by night,
To live life as pleasure, he loathes.
Wisdom is keeping apart from the rational.   430
Grant me instead what the simple believe.

119

Enter SERVANT *and* DIONYSOS.

SERVANT. Pentheus. Lord Pentheus.

Enter PENTHEUS.

We've caught the prey you sent us after.
Here he is, tame enough.
He made no attempt to escape,
Never turned a hair. He didn't turn pale,
But stood there with a smile on his face
And told us to bring him here. He held out his hands.

440   It made my job easier, but I felt a bit ashamed.
So I told him so. 'It's not up to me, friend,' I said,
'Pentheus sent me.' And then there are those Bacchants
You had locked up in the public gaol.
They've gone. They got free,
And now they're leaping about in the fields
Calling upon their Bromios. The chains fell off them.
The doors unbolted themselves without a hand laid on
                      them.

This man, well, I tell you. There's some funny things
Going on in Thebes, and he's the cause,

450   Though it's up to you to decide what to do about it.

PENTHEUS. You're losing your wits, the whole pack of you.
Now I've got my hands on him, he'll not get away in a
                      hurry.

So, my friend. You're not so bad-looking, I see,
Not as far as women are concerned,
Which is why you came to Thebes, no doubt.
Such long hair. Not a wrestler, I think. All down your
                      cheeks.

Very luscious. How pale you are. Not much in the sun,
Are you? Under cover mostly, hunting Aphrodite?
Right then. We'll start with where you come from.

460 DIONYSOS. That's easy enough though nothing to boast of.
Have you ever heard of Tmolos of the flowers?

PENTHEUS. I've heard of it, the area round Sardis.

DIONYSOS. That is where I come from. I'm a Lydian.

PENTHEUS. And these rites you bring to Greece, where do they
                      come from?

DIONYSOS. Dionysos, the son of Zeus, initiated me.

PENTHEUS. You have your own Zeus, do you, who spawns
new gods?

DIONYSOS. There is only one Zeus, Semele's husband.

PENTHEUS. And were you awake when this Dionysos
  Forced himself upon you, or was it a dream?

DIONYSOS. I confronted him face to face. He looked at me
  And gave me his mysteries.   470

PENTHEUS. Ah yes, mysteries. What sort of mysteries would
they be?

DIONYSOS. They are secret except to initiates.

PENTHEUS. Then what are the benefits for his devotees?

DIONYSOS. Considerable, but you may not be told them.

PENTHEUS. You're trying to intrigue me.

IONYSOS. These mysteries are not for the unbeliever.

PENTHEUS. You say you've had a good look at this god.
What's he like?

DIONYSOS. Whatever he wishes. I cannot tell him how to
appear.

PENTHEUS. That's no kind of answer.

DIONYSOS. Any fool finds wisdom foolish.   480

PENTHEUS. Is this the first place you have introduced this god?

DIONYSOS. His rites are danced everywhere abroad.

PENTHEUS. Where they have less control of their senses than
us Greeks.

DIONYSOS. Perhaps more. Practices differ.

PENTHEUS. These practices. Do you practise by day or at
night?

DIONYSOS. Mainly at night. Devotion needs the dark.

PENTHEUS. So does corrupting women.

DIONYSOS. That can be done in daylight.

PENTHEUS. You'll pay for this disgusting sophistry.

DIONYSOS. And you for your mindless irreverence.   490

PENTHEUS. Really. Very brave, this Bacchant, quite a juggler
with words.

DIONYSOS. Tell me my fate. What terrible punishment lies in
store for me?

PENTHEUS. I shall start by cutting off your curls.

DIONYSOS. My hair is sacred, dressed for the god.

121

PENTHEUS. Then there's your thyrsos. Hand it over.
DIONYSOS. It belongs to Dionysos. You take it.
PENTHEUS. You, we'll chain up inside.
DIONYSOS. The god will free me whenever he wants.
PENTHEUS. Very fine with your Bacchants all around you.
DIONYSOS. Take care. He came with me and sees what I

500   suffer.

PENTHEUS. Where exactly would he be, may I ask?
    He is not immediately apparent to my eyes.
DIONYSOS. With me. To a blasphemer invisible.
PENTHEUS. He mocks me. He mocks Thebes. Tie him up.
DIONYSOS. I give you fair warning. It would be unwise to bind

                                                                                  me.

PENTHEUS. We shall soon see who has the power here.
DIONYSOS. You see nothing. Not what you do, what you are,

                                                              who you are.

PENTHEUS. That I can tell you. Pentheus, son of Agauë and

                                                              Echion.

DIONYSOS. Pentheus, an ill-omened name. It suits you.

510 PENTHEUS. Take him down. Put him in the stables.
    He can dance in the dark in there.
    As for this pack of followers he brought with him,
    I'll sell them or set them to work sewing
    Instead of making all this din.
DIONYSOS. As you wish. I cannot suffer what I may not.
    He will repay you for your behaviour, Dionysos,
    Whose existence you deny.
    When you place a restriction on me
    It is Dionysos you affront.
    Exeunt DIONYSOS, SERVANT *and* PENTHEUS.
CHORUS. Dirke, maiden, mistress.
    Acheloös' daughter,

520   Once you kept Zeus' son
    Safe in your spring water.
    In his thigh Zeus placed him,
    Snatched him from the pyre.
    'Enter my male womb,
    Safe from deathless fire.'
    Bacchios. Dionysos.

Dirke, blessed mistress,   530
Why reject me now?
Why disown my worship,
The garlands on my brow?
Why do you oppress me?
This I swear, one day
You'll accept the worship
Which you now deny.
Bromios. Dionysos.

Dragon-seed Pentheus betrays his birth,   540
True son of Echion, sprung from the earth.
Hardly a human, so savage a creature,
God-fighting giant, bloody in feature.
There where our leader lies in the gloom,
Bromios' servant he seeks to entomb.
Do you see from Olympos our witnesses' plight?   550
Come and protect us from tyranny's might.

Where Dionysos? Carrying the thyrsos?
On beast-haunted Nysa, in shade of Olympos?
On crest of Korykia? Where Dionysos?

There he lingers, there he lingers,   560
There where, charming beast in tree-lined glade,
Charming forest, Orpheus played.
You Bromios reveres, blessed Pieria:
Dancing he comes, here he comes prancing,
Never grows weary.   570

From the land of fine horses
Across Axios and Lydia,
From the land of fine waters
He hastens, he hastens
Our Mainad leader.
DIONYSOS (*within*). Ahhh, Bacchae. Hear me, Bacchae. Hear
                                                my voice.
CHORUS. Who? Where? A shout. A cry.
    His. Whose? Calling. Who?
DIONYSOS (*within*). Hear me, Bacchae. I call again.   580

It is I, Bacchae, son of Semele, son of Zeus.

CHORUS. Dionysos. Master. Dionysos. Join us.
Lead us, Dionysos.
Welcome. Bromios, Dionysos.

DIONYSOS (*within*). Come, earthquake, come.
Shake the world to its roots.

CHORUS. Help us. Look. Look there. There.
The palace of Pentheus. See how it shakes.
Shaking to pieces. It falls. The palace is falling.

590   Dionysos within. Worship him. Worship.
We revere. We revere.
Look at the stones, the pillars, the beams.
Bromios cries and the whole house replies.

DIONYSOS (*within*). Lightning bolt! Flashing fire!
Engulf and consume all Pentheus' domain.

CHORUS. See how it blazes. Blazing fire
Licking over the holy tomb. Over Semele's tomb,
Semele, blasted by thunderbolt, thunderbolt of Zeus.

600   Fling yourself earthwards. Fling yourself fearfully.
Cast down your bodies. Fall down, you Mainads.
All-overturning, Zeus' child breaks the house down.
Enter DIONYSOS.

DIONYSOS. Women, outsiders. Were you so terror-stricken
You fell to the ground? I do believe you may have noticed
How Dionysos wobbled the palace of Pentheus.
Up you get. Calm yourselves.
There, that's better.

CHORUS. Light of our light, lord of our Bacchic rites,
We're overjoyed to see you,
So desolate have we been.

610   DIONYSOS. You lost heart, did you, believing
I had fallen into one of Pentheus' dark traps?

CHORUS. How could we help it? What protection was left us?
But how are you free from that vile man's authority?

DIONYSOS. Saving myself was really no problem.

CHORUS. Your hands were tied, bound with chains.

DIONYSOS. I made a fool of him. He thought he had tied me
                                     up,

124

But he never touched me. Delusion.
By the stable, when he thought he was securing me,
He trussed up a bull, shin and hoof.
It was he who snorted all the while,   620
And gnawed his lips, sweat pouring off him,
As I stood quietly by, surveying the scene.
Then came Dionysos to burn up house and tomb.
When the king saw that, he ran about
Shouting at servants to fetch water.
They were all too busy, slaving away . . . naturally,
To no avail. Deciding that I had escaped,
He changed tack, grabbed a sword and rushed indoors.
Dionysos, or so I suppose – this is only what I assume
                                                happened –
Fashioned a phantom inside the house.   630
Pentheus made straight for it, this ethereal, shining thing,
Thinking to kill me. Dionysos mocked him even more,
Razing the house to the ground. He turned it upside down.
That will teach him to tie me up.
Pentheus dropped his sword when he saw that.
A man daring to take on a god. Imagine!
As for me, I simply slipped out here to you.
Pentheus is nothing. I think I hear him coming.
What will he have to say, I wonder?
Not that his bluster upsets me greatly.
Controlling one's temper is a sign of a wise man.   640
    Enter PENTHEUS.
PENTHEUS. This is humiliating. That foreigner
    Chained as he was a minute ago, he's got away.
    So, the fellow's here, is he? What is all this?
    How did you get out? What do you think you're doing
    Standing here in front of my house?
DIONYSOS. Don't take it too hard. And don't come any closer.
PENTHEUS. How did you get out?
DIONYSOS. Did I not tell you that someone would free me?
    Perhaps you were not listening.
PENTHEUS. What someone? Give a straight answer, can't you? 650
DIONYSOS. The god who grew the clustering vine for mortals.

125

PENTHEUS. That, I suppose, is a Dionysiac benefit.

DIONYSOS. You can bear witness to his presence here.

PENTHEUS. I'll have every gate in the walls bolted.

DIONYSOS. To what end? Cannot a god jump over a wall?

PENTHEUS. So clever, aren't you? But maybe not that clever.

DIONYSOS. That clever, certainly. Born wise.

Enter FIRST MESSENGER.

Perhaps you should pay attention to this messenger
And what he has to say. Don't worry. I'll not run off.

660 MESSENGER. Pentheus, Lord of Thebes. I come from Kithairon
Where the snow can fall so thick and white . . .

PENTHEUS. Do you have any news or don't you?

MESSENGER. Bacchants. That is what I've seen,
Rushing about like mad things.
Barefoot. All over the place.
I tell you, my lord, they're amazing,
These things they get up to.
Do you want everything or the edited version?

670 To tell the truth, my lord,
I'm a bit worried how you'll take it.

PENTHEUS. Tell me it all. You'll come to no harm from me.
I have no need to take out my temper
On decent people. The worse the tale you have to tell
About these Bacchants, the more severe
My punishment for their corruption will be.

MESSENGER. It was soon after daybreak, the sun just getting
warm.
My cattle were heading for the tops when I saw them,

680 Three groups of these dancing women.
Autonoë was the leader of one group,
Your mother, Agauë, the second, Ino the third.
They were all fast asleep, stretched out,
Some reclining on pine branches,
Others amongst the oak leaves.
They were lying anywhere, but decently,
No sign of the drink and music you had led us to expect.
No debauchery in the bushes.
Then your mother, when she heard my cattle lowing,

126

Gave a great shout, and jumped up 690
In the middle of the others crying
'Rouse your bodies from sleep.'
And they all threw off their sleepiness
And stood upright, old and young,
Married and unmarried, a marvellous sight.
They let down their hair, tied up their fawnskins
Where they had become disarranged,
And hung on their dappled fur snakes
Which licked their cheeks. Some young ones,
With milk at the breast, their newborn babes deserted, 700
Nursed gazelles or fed young cubs instead.
Then they dressed their hair with ivy,
Oak or flowering briony.
One struck her thyrsos on a rock
And a stream of water flowed out.
Another planted hers in the ground.
That one sprayed out god-given wine. 710
Those who required milk had only to scratch in the earth
And milk poured out. Their ivy wands dripped honey.
I tell you, if you'd been there,
If you'd seen all this, you would be praying
To the god you now pour scorn upon.

We got together, herdsmen and shepherds,
Arguing about all these wonderful things.
Some clever fellow, no countryman,
Made an announcement.
'How about it, men of the hills? 720
Shall we hunt down Agauë, the king's mother,
Out of these revels, and do our lord a favour?'
It seemed like a good idea,
So we laid an ambush in the brush and waited.
In no time at all, they all started shaking their wands,
Shouting to Iacchos, calling on Bromios, son of Zeus.
And the whole mountain went wild for Dionysos,
Animals too. They began to run. Everything ran.
Agauë came leaping past where I was hiding.
I tried to grab her but she let out a scream. 730

127

'Hounds, my swift hounds.
They are hunting us. Men.
Arm with your thyrsi. Arm. Follow me.'
And we fled.
They'd have torn us to pieces, these Bacchants.

They turned instead on our herds where they were feeding.
With her bare hands your own mother
Wrenched and tore at a bellowing cow.
740 Others ripped at calves, stripping them.
Hooves torn off. Ribs wherever you looked.
Pieces of flesh hanging bloody from the trees,
Dripping.
Even bulls, with pride of horn,
Were dragged down,
Set upon by dozens of girlish hands,
Which grabbed at them, defleshing them,
As quickly as you could wink, my lord.
Then off they sprinted, swift as birds,
750 Down to the fertile Theban plain,
To Hysia and Erythrai beneath Kithairon.
Like enemies they invaded, scattering everything.
Snatched children out of houses,
Slung them over their shoulders where they stuck fast,
As did anything they carried,
Even iron and steel, nothing falling to earth.
They bore fire in their hair.
It didn't even scorch them.
The villagers, meanwhile, furious at the raid,
760 Fell to arms. But there's another mystery, my lord.
The steel javelins of the villagers
Didn't so much as draw blood,
But the thyrsi cast by the Bacchants
Wounded them and put them to flight.
Men, routed by women, but not without the help of a god.
Then they went back where they'd come from,
To the fountains the god had raised up for them.
They washed off the blood,
While snakes licked clean their cheeks.

This god, my lord, whoever he is,   770
Accept him in the city.
His power is phenomenal, greater even than I have told
                  you.
  He is the one, as they say, who gives us wine
  To ease our ills. And without wine, there's no love either,
  And precious little else for a man to enjoy.
CHORUS. I hesitated to speak of freedom before such a tyrant,
  But speak I must. Second to no god is our god,
  Dionysos.
PENTHEUS. It is upon us already, spreading like wildfire,
  This Bacchanalian frenzy. The whole of Greece   780
  Will be jeering at us. We must act.
  You, go to the Elektran gate. I want the shield-carriers,
  The cavalry and bowmen. Fast riders, the best shots.
  We march against the Bacchae. It's past all enduring
  To put up with these women's conduct.
DIONYSOS. Pentheus, you take no notice of what I say.
  I have suffered at your hands,
  But I am giving you fair warning.
  Do not bear arms against a god.
  Calm down. Dionysos will never allow you   790
  To drive his followers from the mountains.
PENTHEUS. Don't give me orders. You're free. Isn't that
                  enough?
  Or are you looking for further punishment?
DIONYSOS. It seems to me you would do better to offer him a
                  sacrifice
  Rather than get so excited. You cannot fight
  Against the inevitable, mortal against immortal.
PENTHEUS. I'll offer a sacrifice all right . . . all those women.
  In the woods of Kithairon they'll get the sacrifice they
                  deserve.
DIONYSOS. You will simply run away, even with metal shields
  Against wooden thyrsi. And you will all look rather foolish.
PENTHEUS. I've had enough of this foreigner.   800
  Nothing I do or say will stop his mouth.
DIONYSOS. My friend, listen to me.

129

This still could be turned to your advantage.
PENTHEUS. What can I do? I cannot let my subjects
Overrule me, women at that.
DIONYSOS. I'll bring the women back, unharmed.
PENTHEUS. You're plotting something.
DIONYSOS. Why should I be plotting anything
Beyond using my skill to assist you?
PENTHEUS. You're in this together, plotting
To install this religion here.
DIONYSOS. Why yes, I am. I am in this together with a god.
PENTHEUS. That's enough from you. Fetch me my armour.
DIONYSOS. One thing more. You would like to watch them
810   Up there in the mountains, wouldn't you?
PENTHEUS. Watch them? Why, yes. I'd pay
Good money to see what they are up to.
DIONYSOS. Why this great desire to see them?
PENTHEUS. There's no great pleasure in watching women
                                    drunk.
DIONYSOS. But you would like to take a look, pleasant sight or
                                      not.
PENTHEUS. Yes I would. As long as I was sitting quietly
Out of the way among the trees.
DIONYSOS. They'd sniff you out if you tried to watch them
                                  furtively.
PENTHEUS. That's very true. Out in the open then.
DIONYSOS. Do you want me to show you a way? Is that what
                               you want?
PENTHEUS. Yes. You show me the way. Now, I want to go
820   now.
DIONYSOS. You'll have to put on a dress. Linen, something
                                like that.
PENTHEUS. Dress? What do you mean? Dress like a woman?
DIONYSOS. They'd murder a man if they saw him, now
                                wouldn't they?
PENTHEUS. Yes, of course. You're right. You've thought it all
                                out.
DIONYSOS. Call it inspiration. From Dionysos.
PENTHEUS. A clever idea. Now what?

DIONYSOS. Come indoors. I'll help you get dressed.
PENTHEUS. I don't think I've the nerve. Not dressed like a
                                                woman.
DIONYSOS. Do you want a peep at the Mainads, or do you
                                                not?
PENTHEUS. A dress, you say? What sort of a dress?   830
DIONYSOS. A full-length dress. And a wig, a long one.
PENTHEUS. Any other kind of decoration?
DIONYSOS. You ought to have a headband.
PENTHEUS. Is that everything?
DIONYSOS. Yes, except for a thyrsos and fawnskin.
PENTHEUS. Dress up as a woman? I couldn't do it.
DIONYSOS. The alternative is bloodshed and a battle against
                                                the Bacchae.
PENTHEUS. All right. I'll do it. I have to see them before
                                                anything else.
DIONYSOS. Far more sensible than countering one evil with
                                                another.
PENTHEUS. How will I cross the city without being recognised?   840
DIONYSOS. We'll use quiet roads. I'll take you.
PENTHEUS. Rather than have those Bacchants
   Laugh at me. I'll go inside. I want to think about it.
DIONYSOS. As you wish. I'm ready, whatever you decide.
PENTHEUS. I'll go then. I'll go and prepare my weapons.
   Either that, or do what you suggest.
   Exit PENTHEUS.
DIONYSOS. Straight into the trap. Where he will find,
   Oh my women, his Bacchants and a death sentence.
   Dionysos, close at hand, now it is up to you.
   We will pay him out, but first befuddle his wits,
   Make him mad. Never in his right mind
   Would he put on a dress. Possessed, he will.   850
   After all those dire threats of his,
   I want Thebes helpless with laughter
   As he prinks,
   Ladylike, through the streets.
   I will go and help him
   Into the shroud he must wear

131

When his mother tears him apart.
He will discover, at first hand,
860 Dionysos, son of Zeus,
Most fearful of gods by nature, though the mildest too.
Exit DIONYSOS.
CHORUS. I long to dance through the night without sleeping,
Barefoot,
Neck stretched up to the dew-dropping air,
Like a fawn as she plays in the field,
Fear flown,
Flight-free,
Escaped from the hunter's snare,
870 Where she strained as she strove as she ran,
Past meadow,
Past stream,
Till she found forest peace, far from man.

Where is the beginning of wisdom?
What gift of the gods could be finer for man
Than to raise up his hand o'er the head of his foe,
880 Triumphant?
Nothing finer,
Delightful.

The power of the gods proceeds slowly but surely,
Chastening
The insensitive,
Those whose mad arrogance trusts only itself.
Hidden away lie the traps for the godless.
Time passes,
Slowfoot.
890 The gods have good time to await the unwary.
We must know and must care for the custom of ages,
What's right and what's natural.
These the ideals that religion gives sanction to.

Where is the beginning of wisdom?
What gift of the gods could be finer for man
Than to raise up his hand o'er the head of his foe,
900 Triumphant?

132

Nothing finer.
Delightful.

Happy the man who escapes the sea's tempest.
Peace,
A haven he finds,
Delivered from hardship.
One achieves one thing, another another,
Fortune and happiness,
Hope upon hope.
So to thousands of men may be myriad ambitions.
Some may achieve while others fall backward.
Happy the man who can daily progress.   910
Enter DIONYSOS.
DIONYSOS. Pentheus, so keen to see what you ought not to

                              see,
Come out, Pentheus, out from your palace.
Let's have a look at you, tricked out like a Bacchant
To go and spy on your mother and her troupe.
Enter PENTHEUS, dressed as a woman.
There now, every inch a daughter of Kadmos.
PENTHEUS. I can see two suns, I think,
And the seven-gated city of Thebes, double.
A bull. I think you look like a bull,   920
Horns on your head? A wild animal.
Did you used to be an animal? You've become a bull.
DIONYSOS. The god is with us.
He was ill-disposed before, but now he has joined us.
You are seeing what you ought to see.
PENTHEUS. Who do I look like? Ino, surely,
Though perhaps more like my mother, Agauë?
DIONYSOS. Their living image. You could be either one.
Wait. A lock of hair is out of place.
Tuck it back in the hood where I set it.
PENTHEUS. I must have loosened it   930
When I was shaking my head about, Bacchant-fashion.
DIONYSOS. Let me be your dresser. Keep your head still.
                                      There.
PENTHEUS. Set me to rights. I am in your hands now.

133

DIONYSOS. The girdle could be tighter, and your dress
   Doesn't hang quite right at the ankle.
PENTHEUS. I see. On the right. The left's all right, though,
                                       isn't it?
DIONYSOS. How you will thank me when you finally see the
940   Bacchants
   And find out that you are wrong about them.
PENTHEUS. What's the right way to hold a thyrsos? This hand,
                                     is it?
   I want to be like a real Bacchant.
DIONYSOS. Right hand, and you raise your right foot in time.
   Good, that's it. I do commend this change of heart.
PENTHEUS. I wonder if I could lift up Kithairon
   On my shoulders, and all the Bacchae with it.
DIONYSOS. Anything you like. Your wits were distracted
                                   before.
   Now they are sound again.
PENTHEUS. What about taking a crowbar? Or shall I just
   Put a shoulder against the cliffs
950   And heave them over, with brute force?
DIONYSOS. You do not want to do any harm
   To the holy places of the nymphs, now do you,
   Or the haunts of Pan which echo with his pipes?
PENTHEUS. No, of course. And it would never be right to use
                                     force
   Against a woman. I'll hide in the trees.
DIONYSOS. You will find the right hiding-place
   For someone who wants to peer at the Bacchae.
PENTHEUS. I can see them already in the bushes,
   At it, like sparrows.
960 DIONYSOS. That is why you are going – as a watchdog.
   Perhaps you will catch them. Unless they catch you first.
PENTHEUS. Take me through the centre of Thebes
   As I am the only man with the nerve to go.
DIONYSOS. You bear responsibility for Thebes, all by yourself.
   You alone. Your trial awaits. Follow me.
   I will deliver you safely. Someone else will return you.
PENTHEUS. My mother.

134

DIONYSOS. For everyone to see.
PENTHEUS. That is why I am going.
DIONYSOS. You will be carried back . . .
PENTHEUS. In triumph.
DIONYSOS. In your mother's arms.
PENTHEUS. You will ruin me.
DIONYSOS. You could say that.
PENTHEUS. Not that I don't deserve it.   970
    Exit PENTHEUS.
DIONYSOS. What a remarkable man you are,
    But you face an ordeal so remarkable
    It will bring you fame in heaven.
    Such an ordeal and so young a man.
    But I will win. You will see. Bromios and I will win.
    Exit DIONYSOS.
CHORUS. Go. Swift. Hounds. Madness.
    Sting. Madness. Sting.
    Kadmos' daughters,
    Madness, sting.   980
    Mainad decked out as female.

    Mother spies. Spy from rock or spy from tree.
    'Spy, Bacchae, racing Bacchae.'
    Spy's mother. 'No, women.
    Lion-cub. Gorgon-spawn.'   990

    Sword of Justice, sword through throat
    Of the godless, lawless, worthless man.

    Echion's son, stung with madness,
    Fighting your mysteries, Dionysos.
    And his mother's. Fights from weakness,   1000
    Crazed with daring, fighting mysteries.

    Carefree life? Behave like mortals.
    Cleverness for the clever. I choose better.
    Reverence, honour, respect for the gods,
    These man should practise by day and by night.

    Sword of Justice, sword through throat   1010
    Of the godless, lawless, worthless man.

135

Come, Dionysos, appear as a bull,
As a many-mouthed dragon,
As a fire-breathing lion.

1020   Come, Bacchios. Come, Bacchios.
Hunt, mock, trap, Bacchios.
Pursue him, sneer at him, snare him,
The man who would chase your Mainads.
Collapsed at their feet
He will find what he looked for.
Enter SECOND MESSENGER.
MESSENGER. Nothing but grief. I'm only a slave
But I grieve for my masters, as a good slave must.
This family, till now so prosperous throughout Greece,
Family of Kadmos, the dragon-seed sower . . . grief . . .
CHORUS. Tell us. What news of the Bacchae?
1030 MESSENGER. The son of Echion, Pentheus. Dead.
CHORUS. Dionysos, lord, you show your true face.
Great is the god Dionysos.
MESSENGER. What? What are you saying, women?
You rejoice at this family's disaster?
CHORUS. No family of mine. I am free to sing my foreign
                                    songs,
Safe from the fear of restraint.
MESSENGER. Thebes has men enough . . .
CHORUS. Dionysos is my master, not Thebes, Dionysos.
MESSENGER. Maybe so, but even you should not rejoice
1040   At such terrible things. It can't be right.
CHORUS. Tell me. The whole story. How did he die,
This evil worker of evil deeds?
MESSENGER. We left the last cottages of Thebes behind,
And crossed the Asopos, heading for Kithairon.
Just Pentheus, me following my master,
And that foreigner to show us the way.
As soon as we got there we crouched down
In a grassy hollow to watch, silent and unseen.
1050   There's a rift between tall cliffs,
Waterfalls running down them,
All shaded by pine-trees.

That's where we saw the Mainads, hard at work, but
content.
Some were decorating thyrsi with sprigs of new ivy.
Others sang Bacchic songs to one another,
Frisking, free as colts.
Pentheus couldn't see the whole company
And he said, poor man,
'I cannot get a proper look from here
At these self-styled Mainads. 1060
If I could climb up higher,
In one of those pines perhaps,
I could get a decent look at this debauchery of theirs.'
Then I saw the foreigner do a remarkable thing.
He took hold of a soaring branch of one of the pines,
And he pulled it, pulled it right down to the dark earth.
He bent it over like a bow or the curved felloe on a wheel.
Just so did this strange man take that tree
In his two hands, and bend it to the ground.
No ordinary man could have done it.
His strength was superhuman. 1070
He sat Pentheus astride the branches,
And let the tree slowly straighten,
Taking care not to unseat him.
Up it went, up towards the sky, my master on its back,
For all the Mainads to see, plainer than he saw them.
No sooner was Pentheus up there in full view
Than the foreigner disappeared and a voice
Came out of the air, as it were the voice of Dionysos.
'Ladies,' he cried, 'here is the man
Who would make mock of us and our mysteries. 1080
I offer him to you for punishment.'
He spoke and a blinding flash of fire
Struck earth from heaven.
Everything went quite still, air, trees, animals even,
Quite still.
The Mainads got to their feet,
Some having missed his words,
And stared about them. He called again.

137

This time Kadmos' daughters realised what he required.
1090 And they ran.
They ran, swift as birds,
Agauë, her sisters, all of them,
Over river and rock, mad,
For the god had breathed on them.
Then they saw my master perched in his tree.
They hurled stones at first and sticks,
Climbing the cliff opposite.
1100 Some threw thyrsi at their wretched target.
He was too high even for their frenzy,
But could only sit there appalled.
They snatched off branches from the oaks
To lever up his pine, but their efforts bore no fruit.
Then Agauë spoke.
'Circle the trunk, Mainads, grasp it.
We need to catch this clamberer
Before he reveals god's dances.'
Dozens of hands hauled at the tree,
1110 Then heaved it out of the earth.
Down fell Pentheus,
Down to the ground with an awful cry.
He knew now what was happening.
His mother started it, the ritual slaughter.
Desperate Agauë. As she fell upon him,
He tore off the headdress so she would recognise him
And grabbed her cheek.
'Mother, it's me. It's Pentheus, your son.
Pity me. I've done no wrong.
1120 Don't kill me.' But her eyes were rolling.
She was frothing, imagining god knows what
In her Dionysiac frenzy.
She ignored his words, and took his left hand in hers,
Planted a foot in his ribs
And ripped off his arm at the shoulder.
Her strength was supernatural.
Ino set to work on the other side,
Tearing out handfuls of flesh,

138

And Autonoë and the whole mob of Bacchants.   1130
A single terrible scream,
Pentheus' agony, their exultation.
One ran off with an arm, another a foot still in its shoe.
His ribs were stripped to the bone.
Bright red hands toyed with lumps of flesh.
The remains were strewn about,
By the rocks, in the undergrowth, anywhere.
We'll never find them.
But the head, the poor head,
His mother chanced to snatch it up,   1140
And stuck it on her thyrsos.
She left her sisters dancing away
And set off through Kithairon,
Brandishing the head as though it were a mountain lion's.
She arrived in the city glorying in her frightful trophy,
Shrieking about her splendid Dionysos,
Fellow-huntsman, victorious. A victory of tears.
I can't stay to see this sight,
Not Agaue's homecoming.
Balance. Reason. That's all we can aim for.   1150
Honour the gods and stick to that.
Exit MESSENGER.
CHORUS. Dionysos, we dance for you,
   Call on your name, Dionysos.
   Dionysos, we praise you.
   Defeat for the dragon-born,
   Dragon-spawn Pentheus,
   Dressed like a woman,
   Sporting his thyrsos,
   Flaunting his death-warrant,
   Led by the bull-god, Dionysos.

   You've achieved a famous victory,   1160
   Bacchants of Kadmos,
   A victory for suffering,
   A victory for tears.
   Fine victory for a mother,
   Paddling in her own child's blood.

139

And here I see her, the mother of Pentheus,
Wild-eyed Agauë. Welcome to our revelling company.
Enter AGAUË.

AGAUË. Bacchae from Asia.

CHORUS. You call? Ahhh.

1170 AGAUË. See what I've brought home from the mountains.
The garlands are quite fresh. Happy hunting.

CHORUS. Fellow-reveller, I see you and welcome you.

AGAUË. Look. My lion-cub, caught without a trap.

CHORUS. Where did you find it?

AGAUË. On Kithairon.

CHORUS. Kithairon?

AGAUË. Kithairon killed him.

CHORUS. Who was the first to . . .

AGAUË. I was. Fortunate Agauë. That's what they're calling
1180   me.

CHORUS. Any others?

AGAUË. Kadmos' daughters.

CHORUS. Kadmos'?

AGAUË. They fingered the prey. But after me. After me.
Good luck in the hunt. Will you share the feast with me?

CHORUS. Share, poor woman, share?

AGAUË. Just a cub. Soft mane and downy whiskers.

CHORUS. Mane, yes, and whiskers.

1190 AGAUË. Dionysos himself, clever hunter, set us onto our prey.

CHORUS. Our lord, the hunter.

AGAUË. Have I done well?

CHORUS. Of course. Very well.

AGAUË. Soon all the men of Thebes . . .

CHORUS. And Pentheus, your son, Pentheus.

AGAUË. He'll be pleased with his mother for capturing such a
                                                                                            lion-cub.

CHORUS. A rare prize.

AGAUË. Rare is right.

CHORUS. Are you pleased?

AGAUË. Ecstatic.
Anyone can see what a fine creature I have bagged.

1200 CHORUS. Show it then. Show everyone this trophy,

140

Poor woman, this trophy you bring.

AGAUË. Citizens of our dear Thebes, draw near
And examine the spoil. We, Kadmos' daughters,
Have captured it without spear or net.
With just our white fingers.
So much for the boasting of men and their weaponry.
This creature we dismembered with our bare hands.
Where's my old father? Send for him.   1210
And Pentheus. Where's my son, Pentheus?
He should climb up with this lion's head
And nail it over the door.

Enter KADMOS, *attended.*

KADMOS. Follow me in. Bring him here,
Here in front of his own house –
What's left of him. Poor Pentheus.
I found his body spread over Kithairon,
All torn, in pieces.
I found something in the wood . . .   1220
I was on my way back from revelling
With old Teiresias when they told me
What my daughters had done.
I went back to the mountain and found the boy.
The Bacchae had . . . killed him.
Aktaion's mother, Autonoë was there.
Ino too, in among the oak groves, still raving.
But someone told me that Agauë
Had wandered back here in her mania.
How right they were. I cannot look.   1230

AGAUË. Father. Now you can be proud of us.
What daughters you have sired,
The best in the world.
And especially me.
I've given up weaving for hunting,
And with my bare hands.
Look here. No, what I'm holding in my arms,
A trophy to mount on the palace walls.
Here, take hold of it, father,
And let's call our friends to a celebration.   1240

141

They'll think well of you for this.

KADMOS. No man could measure the horror of what I see.
Murder, vile murder, at those frightful hands.
This is the victim you want Thebes to celebrate.
My grief is for you. For me too.
A just revenge? No, too cruel.
Dionysos is one of our family,
1250 But he has destroyed our house.

AGAUĒ. How grumpy an old man can get,
Looking at me like that.
I want my son to take after his mother,
Race to the hunt with the young men of Thebes.
All he does is fight gods.
You should put him right, father. It's your place.
Call him here, someone,
So he can see how well I have done.

KADMOS. Oh my dear. When you realise what you've done,
1260 Your pain will be unbearable. Madness
Is the best that you can hope for.

AGAUĒ. What's wrong? Why so solemn?

KADMOS. Look up. Look at the sky.

AGAUĒ. What am I meant to be looking at?

KADMOS. Is it the same as before, or do you see a change?

AGAUĒ. It's brighter, perhaps, a little clearer.

KADMOS. And the confusion in your mind. Is that still with
you?

AGAUĒ. I don't understand. I was confused.
1270 But that seems to be passing.

KADMOS. Can you hear what I'm saying? Tell me if you can.

AGAUĒ. What were we talking about, father? I can't remember.

KADMOS. What family was it you married into?

AGAUĒ. You gave me to Echion, the one they call the dragon-
spawn.

KADMOS. Yes, and the son you bore your husband?

AGAUĒ. Pentheus. Our son is Pentheus.

KADMOS. And whose . . . whose head is that you're cradling in
your arms?

AGAUĒ. A lion's. That's what the hunters told me.

142

KADMOS. Look at it. No, fully. Look.

AGAUË. What is it? What am I holding? 1280

KADMOS. Look again. Carefully. Now do you realise?

AGAUË. What I see is unbearable. God help me.

KADMOS. Is it anything like a lion?

AGAUË. God help me. The head is Pentheus.

KADMOS. We wept. We knew. You never realised.

AGAUË. Who killed him? Why am I carrying this?

KADMOS. The truth is terrible. Best not to know.

AGAUË. Tell me. My heart is pounding. I have to know.

KADMOS. You killed him. You and your sisters. You killed
him.

AGAUË. Where? At home? Somewhere else? 1290

KADMOS. There, where his own hounds ripped Aktaion to
pieces.

AGAUË. Whatever was the poor boy doing on Kithairon?

KADMOS. He went to make fun of your Dionysos and his rites.

AGAUË. Our Dionysos? What were we doing there?

KADMOS. You didn't know what you were doing. The whole
city was deranged.

AGAUË. Now I see it. Dionysos has destroyed us.

KADMOS. He was slighted. You slighted him, denying his
divinity.

AGAUË. Where is my son's body, father?

KADMOS. There are the remains. It wasn't easy . . .

AGAUË. The body is . . . all there? 1300

KADMOS. Don't look. The head you have. That is what I
could find.

AGAUË. How did Pentheus get involved in this madness of
mine?

KADMOS. Like you, he disdained the god.
We are all involved in this disaster,
You, the son you see here dead, and me as well.
No male heirs. The family is destroyed.
This house looked up to you, my boy.
My grandson, my support.
They went in awe of you in Thebes. 1310
No one could insult the old man with you around.

143

Or else you made him pay.
Dishonoured I must leave my home,
Kadmos, the great, founder of Thebes,
Sower and reaper of the finest of races.
I loved you most. In death I love you still.
Never again to hug you,
To feel your touch on my cheek, or hear your voice:
'Is something the matter, grandfather?
1320 Is someone upsetting you?
Tell me. I'll soon put a stop to it.'
Now I am desolate, and so are you.
Mother, daughters, pitiful.
If any here cast doubt on supernatural power,
Let him consider this boy's death, and take heed.
CHORUS. Kadmos, you have my pity. Your daughter's child,
He got what he deserved, but the pain is yours.
AGAUË. Father, you see the change in me . . .
[*The manuscript breaks off here. Translator's conjectural
reconstruction:*]
Sane now, I see what I could not see.
My own child, Pentheus.
How did I not know him? My sisters too?
My son's blood is upon their hands,
Loving hands which tore away his life.
And I am left to mourn the son
Who should have mourned for me.
Whose fate is worse?
Here, place the head and cover it. Cover it quickly.
Dionysos was the cause and now I know his power.
What mortal man could stand and face his fury?
Enter DIONYSOS, *above.*
DIONYSOS. *What mortal man, indeed?*
I am Dionysos, son of Zeus and your sister Semele.
I came to Thebes to seek my earthly home.
But how was I received?
The city rejected me. My family cast me out,
Me, a god, they banished from their mortal company.
My mother Semele's sisters I drove mad

144

Up into the mountains,
And they have done what I had them do.
So all of you as exiles must seek your own redemption,
An expiation which only time can bring.
Pentheus, my cousin, who dared to sneer at my rites,
I mocked in my turn, and sent him
Bacchios-mad to where his mother was waiting.
[*Manuscript resumes:*]

For Kadmos, my grandfather, and Harmonia his wife,   1330
A different fate is in store. You shall turn into snakes –
Zeus' oracle has forecast this – and lead great armies.
Strange deeds and in strange places,
With no peace at the last.
Leading barbarian hordes, you will sack cities,
And even Apollo's oracle, though that will bring a grim
                                                                   return.
But Ares, Harmonia's father, will preserve you
And take you eventually to the land of the Blessed.
That is my immortal decree, and I am the son of Zeus,
Dionysos, a good friend to the wise.   1340
A pity you did not realise it sooner.

KADMOS. Dionysos, we implore you. We admit that we were
                                                                   wrong.
DIONYSOS. Too late. You acknowledge me far too late.
KADMOS. We know that, but you are too severe.
DIONYSOS. You offended me, me a god.
KADMOS. A god should not show passion like a man.
DIONYSOS. Zeus agreed to all this long ago.
AGAUË. Come now, father, exile is our fate.   1350
DIONYSOS. Go then. Why put off the inevitable?
KADMOS. We have come to a terrible pass, my child,
  Every one of us, your sisters too.
  I must go and live in foreign lands, an old man
  Fated, with Harmonia, my wife, daughter of Ares,
  To lead an alien army against Greece:
  Changed to a snake, but warlord
  Against the altars and tombs of my country.
  No peace for me until I cross Acheron's stream.

145

1360 AGAUË. I must go too, father, and I must part from you.

KADMOS. Why cling to me, poor child,
  Like a young white swan still clinging to an old?

AGAUË. Where can I turn, cast out from my country?

KADMOS. I don't know, my dear. Your father can't help you
                                                      now.

AGAUË. Farewell. Home, city, country. An exile.

1370 KADMOS. Go to Aristaios. He will protect you.

AGAUË. Father, I feel pity for you.

KADMOS. And I for you. Your sisters too.

AGAUË. This punishment Dionysos has visited on our family.
                                                 It is terrible.

DIONYSOS. What you made me suffer was terrible,
  My name made light of in Thebes.

AGAUË. Father. Farewell.

KADMOS. Farewell, my child. Though what can fare well
1380   mean?

AGAUË. Take me to my sisters, my fellow-exiles.
  I want to go where cursed Kithairon
  Shall never see me more, nor I set eyes on Kithairon.
  Some place where I can forget the thyrsos.
  All that I leave to others.
  Exeunt AGAUË and KADMOS.

CHORUS. However clear they may appear,
  The gods are seldom what they seem.
1390 The unexpected is the theme
  Of the mystery acted here.
  Exeunt DIONYSOS and CHORUS.

A Note on the Translators

DAVID THOMPSON directed his first Greek tragedy, *The Bacchae*, when reading Classics at Oxford. In 1964 he mounted a two-month Euripides season at the Theatre Royal, Stratford East, consisting of *Electra*, *The Trojan Women* and *Iphigeneia in Tauris*, and has also directed *The Bacchae* at the Edinburgh Festival and *Medea* and *The Phoenician Women* at the Greenwich Theatre. His translations include *Electra*, *Medea*, Aeschylus' *Prometheus Bound*, Sophocles' *Oedipus at Colonus* and three plays by Molière. The text of *The Phoenician Women* included in this volume was used for Katie Mitchell's acclaimed production with the Royal Shakespeare Company in the 1996/97 season.

J. MICHAEL WALTON worked in the professional theatre as an actor and director before joining the University of Hull, where he is Professor of Drama. He has published four books on Greek theatre, *Greek Theatre Practice*, *The Greek Sense of Theatre: Tragedy Reviewed*, *Living Greek Theatre: A Handbook of Classical Performance and Modern Production* and *Menander and the Making of Comedy* (with the late Peter Arnott). He edited *Craig on Theatre* and is Series Editor of Methuen Classical Greek Dramatists. He has translated plays by Sophocles, Euripides, Menander and Terence and is Director of the Performance Translation Centre in the Drama Department at the University of Hull.